HOW TO OPEN AND RUN
AN INDEPENDENT
AUTOMOBILE DEALERSHIP

From the Publisher

It is our pleasure to publish and present to you this work, entitled, Race to The Finish Line…How to Operate and Run an Independent Automobile Dealership. We trust you find this book to be a tremendous help to you.

As a matter of full disclosure, we want to insure that you realize the information contained in this book is for educational and informational purposes only. In no way, shape, or form does the publisher promote or assume liability for the content of the book. While we have completed every step possible to validate the material provided by the contributing authors, we cannot be responsible for actions or consequences resulting from use of the information. The reader, and ultimately the implementing party (dealer), are responsible for his/her dealership.

Also, please know that most of the proceeds from this book will be used as a fundraiser for the Carolinas Independent Automobile Dealers Association to promote the well-being of the industry. The authors do not receive royalties directly from the sale of the book.

Thank you again and enjoy this great work.

Waymaker Learning Corporation

Table of Contents

Photos provided courtesy of Buddy Martin

FORWARD

By: Buddy Martin

Eight Time Hall of Famer and Legendary International Auto Drag Racing Champion

From green light to the finish line in National Hot Rod Association (NHRA), Pro-Stock racing can sometimes take just under 6.5 seconds. At over 200 MPH, it seems like a flash. While the race is quick, the journey to get a victory is not always as quick.

When Ronnie Sox and I joined forces in 1962 to form the Sox & Martin Racing Team, we did not blast out of the shoot and go directly to the top. We were very successful, but many factors impacted our ability to win. At the top of that list, was we needed the right people on our team. I knew that the right driver was Ronnie and he believed that I was the right person to take the lead on managing the business. At first, we did not have a lot of help. Ronnie drove the car, we both worked on the car, we drove our hauler to the races on the circuit, and I worked the market for sponsors. However, we quickly prepared a plan to capture the circuit and we worked the plan. Over time we added people to take on many of the duties we were doing and we were able to focus more on critical roles.

It all came at us so fast. In the end, with the right team, a game plan for success, the right resources and a little bit of good fortune, the Sox & Martin Racing Team became the team to beat. As we ended our careers in racing, we enjoyed Hall of Fame honors in most of the industry's top organizations. We each transitioned to new ventures.

For Ronnie, he spent most of his time promoting the brand and the sport until his death about seven years ago.

As for me, I eventually found another way to stay involved in the car business. I opened my own independent automobile dealership in Fayetteville, North Carolina. Just like with my race team, when I started the dealership, I was the only employee. Sometime later I was able to add a part-time secretary, eventually a full-time salesman, and a few years later, I was delighted to have my son join me in the business. Our model was unconventional at the time. We started a Lease Here Pay Here (LHPH) business. I was fortunate to combine funds I saved from racing with a couple of lines of credit from two local banks. We also took on some individual investors to get the funds needed to build a portfolio sufficient to create the revenue we desired. Now 22 years later, we have bought out our investors, purchased property and built a state-of-the-art dealership facility with service bays. Our team of sales staff, finance and insurance professionals, as well as, our top-notch mechanics and detail staff, provides our customers with great vehicles and terrific service.

As you venture to open and run your own independent car dealership, you too will need a plan, the right people, good resources and persistence to be successful. You are on the right track by reading this book. "Race to The Finish Line" is filled with great content from successful dealers and industry leaders. You are wise to consider the advice you will read about in this book. Whether you are a novice or dealer with some experience, this book can be a wonderful resource for you.

I consider it an honor to invite you to get a head start on your competition by reading "Race to The Finish Line." Your success in this business can be as fast as a trip up the drag strip or it may realistically take a bit longer. Either way, the journey is for sure to be more enjoyable and fruitful if you take time to prepare for the race. Couple the preparation with persistence, desire, sacrifice and hard work and you will win a few. The contributing authors of this book want you to be the best. I am confident you will be just that.

An old friend of mine, Jim Griggs, once told me, "The harder I work, the more successful I become." I have found that to be true even today. We learn a lot more from winners than losers and the winners are in this book. So enjoy this book, put it to work today and I will see you at the finish line!

INTRODUCTION

By: Marshall Perry
Independent Automobile Dealer
Past President and Former Chairman of CIADA Executive Committee

When I became an independent automobile dealer more than 50 years ago, there was little regulation and even less competition. Across the years, it became apparent to me that the rules of the game were changing. The state and federal government were both taking notice of the industry and seeking to insure that dealers operated by the law and that consumers were protected from bad business practices. The industry did not enjoy a great reputation back then. It has been an on-going battle to improve the opinion customers have of car dealers.

As I started, I did not have a roadmap or blueprint and very few outlets to help me. I had good counsel from my father, a goal in mind and a heart for providing great service to my customers. With that I ventured out on my own. Looking back, I realize how much easier it would have been if I had had a book like, "Race to The Finish Line" to read and study.

Included in the chapters of this book are insights gleaned from experience, lessons learned from leading dealers and industry experts, and, simply stated, sage counsel for you, the new independent dealer. By reading this book, you will come to understand in more detail some of what will be required to be successful once you have your license. Once you get your dealers license, you will have more questions than you can imagine. Far too many new dealers just take a guess at how to solve an issue or which program to explore. With the help of these contributing authors, you do not have to go it alone. The concepts, theories and practices discussed in this book provide you a laundry list of direction arrows to guide you toward success. Here's just a glimpse of what you will learn.

You will learn how to purchase a car and make a profit on that unit. Providing a warranty on your inventory will help you give confidence to the customer about the car they are purchasing. Better still, selling the customer a vehicle service contract to protect against potential costly repairs after the sale will keep the customer happy and the car running longer. Choosing the right dealership model is very important. In this book, the authors give you information to determine whether you should use the Buy Here Pay Here Model, the Lease Here Pay Here Model, a more conventional retail model with outside financing or operate as a cash dealer. And, of course, you might decide after reading this book to be a wholesale dealer only. The content contained herein is an excellent commentary on the various choices available to you.

What's more, in running your dealership, you will need the right team. Selecting and training sales people is critical to your success. It's easy to talk the sales game, but it is an all together different story when it's game time. You will be excited to learn a sales process that works in this book.

When I began my business, we only needed a title and a bill of sale to conduct a sales transaction; however, today that paperwork process is overbearing. That's why you will want to consider using a dealer management software system to insure you do the paperwork correctly and efficiently. In Race to The Finish Line, you will be exposed to just what to look for in choosing a system that works best for you.

While reading this book, you will be able to explore floor planning concepts and finance options. Additionally, you will be challenged to "begin with the end in mind" as you learn about the need for and the components of a well-defined strategic plan. This process will be drilled down to a point of advising you on creating a business plan to help you acquire funding for your business.

Maintaining compliance with state and federal laws is a big challenge for the independent dealer today. In this book, much emphasis is given to make certain you have a general knowledge of what's required of you and your dealership.

And of course, I would be remiss if I failed to point out that directing you to consider the value of being a member of an industry trade association concludes this book. I can say unequivocally that belonging to the dealers' association helped me immeasurably. With little outside expertise to help me navigate the waters of an ever changing and always challenging industry, without the association, I would have been lost and likely out of business long ago.

Race to The Finish Line…How to Open and Run an Independent Automobile Dealership is a project created by dealers with the success of future dealers in mind. You are in for a treat as you read and experience the rich content of this project. Get ready for a smooth ride to success as you consume the terrific information in this book.

CHAPTER ONE
Begin With The End In Mind
Developing Your Strategic/Business Plan
By Marty Coates

A number of years ago, I was preparing to teach a pre-licensing course to a group of prospective independent automobile dealers in Lexington, South Carolina. As the participants began to file into the classroom and complete their registration, I was at the front of the room setting up my audio-visual equipment. Amidst the noise in the room, I heard one of the participants at the registration table as he was very loud and was asking a lot of questions. From where I was standing, I could tell he was a young man, very tall, and apparently joined at the seminar by another young man who was a bit shorter. The two may have been in their early twenties at best. They hurried up to the front of the classroom and took seats on the first row.

As the class began, I could tell that at least one of these two young men was going to be a trainer's nightmare. While the best of classes should include interaction from the audience, a question at every bullet on every slide was for sure going to make for a long day for everyone. So at an early morning class break, I went to this participant and tried to determine more about him. I asked him, "Tell me, exactly what brings you to this seminar?" He quickly responded, "All my life I have wanted to be a car dealer." (All his life? He was only 21 or 22 years of age). He went on to say, "I got my buddy to join me, (thus the other shorter young man). We put together $2,500 and we are ready to go. We just have to get this class and we are off and running." Well, I did not have the heart to tell him that this was only the beginning, for I could not bring myself to burst their bubble. However, since meeting them, I have told their story as an example to literally thousands of prospective dealers. I call them the Dynamic Duo, the $2,500 Dream Team.

While they have the energy and now, certificates, they are certainly facing some challenges. The independent automobile business is a capital-intensive business today. There was a time when you could start in this business for a small amount of money, but today the game is different. Inventory prices are high, availability of financing options for inventory are not at optimal levels, and the advent of technology allows individuals to shop and others to sell inventory more readily and economically directly to the consumer. So their dream is not too lofty, rather their plan or lack of a plan is the real challenge.

How about you? Have you considered the full scope of your dealership business? Have you taken the time to transfer your grand idea into a workable strategic/business plan?

Today, more than ever before, it is imperative that you have a strategic plan before you take off and open a new business. The days of calling your friend at the bank and getting a line of credit based on your good name and good credit are over. Banks and other lenders require more documentation than ever and will, in most cases, ask for a business plan. Will you have such a plan?

In this chapter, I will share some basic, yet proven components of a well-defined strategic planning process. You will be directed to tools to assist you with taking that strategic plan and further developing a business plan. This takes a bit of work upfront, but will likely yield you much success down the road.

The Strategic Process
The process of developing a strategic plan requires that you have a picture of the success you want to accomplish with your

dealership. From that picture, once verbalized, described and written down, you can begin the process of planning toward it. To get from where you are to where you want to go normally requires a roadmap or Global Positioning System (GPS). But before you begin the journey, you should consider the following:

1) Who are my customers?
2) What will I sell or provide as a company?
3) What is distinctive (competitive advantage) about my product or process of delivery?
4) Why would someone buy from me?

This analysis should continue with an in depth look at you, your team and your organization. Conduct a SWOT Analysis to gather essential pictures of where you are before you start. The acronym SWOT is short for Strengths, Weaknesses, Opportunities and Threats. For example, you may consider your sales force a strength, your collections department a weakness, your service department an opportunity for growth and a new dealership opening across the street as a threat. Spend sufficient time on the SWOT analysis so that you can look deep and wide at your anticipated dealership operations.

With the results of the SWOT analysis in hand, you must begin the process of articulating your vision, confirming your corporate mission and developing a strategy that will get you to where you want to be in the future.

The key components of a Strategic Plan are described below. Take a few moments to read and consider how the development process works.

The first activity is to state a clear picture of your organization at some point in the future (3, 5, or 7 years). This picture is commonly referred to as your Vision. It should be stated as if you are already there. See your company/dealership as you desire it in terms of the number of units you desire to sell each year, the size organization you hope to be, the type of team and level of service you will provide, just to name a few. Remember the vision should be in front of you. It is a place you desire to arrive at some day.

What is your purpose? Why are you in the business you are in? In other words, what is your mission? The **Mission** should define the "why" and the "what" but not the "where." It is foundational, usually answering a need or call, providing a product or service. Your corporate mission does not propel you forward; instead, it holds you up. It is the reason you do what you do. Be careful about writing lengthy, verbose mission statements. The more specifically you can describe your mission the better focused your activities will be. It is difficult for us to truly be all things to all people. Focus on what you do and do it better than anyone else in the business.

In a dynamic organization, there are always things that impact your ability to realize your vision and execute your mission. Some are internal factors while others are external to the organization. **Key Business Drivers (KBD)** are factors you can control. They are key indicators you use to gauge your progress toward your goals and vision. Create a list of questions to be superimposed over the organizational activity at any time. For example, "Do we have the right people on the bus? Do we have enough money in the bank to cover our expenses?" etc.

What about the external factors that you cannot control? What **Critical Success Factors (CSF)** can you identify that might impact your ability to accomplish your vision? In most cases, we cannot stop these from happening, but we may be able to influence how they impact us. By attempting to identify CSFs and prepare contingency plans in the event they arise, we position our organization to weather most challenges. For example, we might identify governmental regulations as a CSF. How do you prepare? How will you respond? Another CSF might be a natural disaster. Do you control the weather? No, but you will need to plan a response to the possibility and how it might impact your business.

Another important factor in plotting the course of your business is setting long-term **Goals** or objectives. Depending on the span of your vision, goals may be set to be accomplished between three to five years. They are more specific and measureable than the vision, but less specific than the strategic objectives that follow. Goals must be developed by using what is called the SMART TEST. Goals should be:
- **Specific**
- **Measurable**
- **Attainable**
- **Realistic**
- **Time-bound**

For example, if you have a target for sales volume aligned with your vision, a goal statement that meets the SMART test might read, "Achieve $200,000 in sales volume by the end of 2017."

In order for you to reach your goals, mid-range targets or **Strategic Objectives** must be accomplished. As you accomplish them the picture of your goals becomes clearer. In most cases, strategic objectives are targets about one to three years out. An example of a written strategic objective might be, " Develop and implement a marketing plan by December 2015."

To accomplish your strategic objectives, you must determine the near-term tasks or **Actions** that will be necessary to realize your vision. Taking shortcuts here will cost you later. Normally, actions are required to be completed within 12 months. These are immediate action steps, for example, "Hire and train one full-time salesperson by June 2014."

The final key component in this process is the establishment of organizational core **Values**. These are our right and left out-of-bound markers. They keep our actions in check. If we move too far right or too far left, our Values bring us back into alignment or help us to realize we have moved away from our core plan. Each organization should prepare its own list of core Values, which best describe its intended internal compass.

Now that we have described the components of the planning process, let's take a look at how the pieces fit together. The strategic planning process is planned backwards, but executed from the bottom up. For example, as you see the model to follow, notice the design of the process- Vision to Actions. We plan the vision first, but we accomplish the vision by tackling the actions, strategic objectives and goals in that order.

The diagram below is a visual representation of the strategic process:

Figure 1.

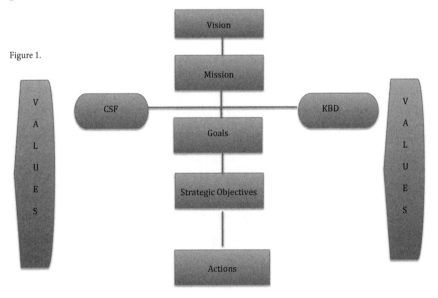

Here are nine keys that summarize the process and help drive you towards success in accomplishing your strategic plan:

1) Clearly state your vision.
2) Institutionalize your corporate mission.
3) Set long-term goals, strategic objectives and near-term actions.
4) Communicate clearly your corporate values.
5) Measure progress along the way.
6) Hold your team accountable.
7) Be flexible and adapt to changes in the plan.
8) Revisit your plan periodically.
9) Celebrate your accomplishments with the team.

With the strategic plan complete, you now have an organizational focus and a plan towards a successful future. To best insure your dealership stays on track with the vision that you have crafted, you must now hold yourself and others accountable to accomplishing the objectives and actions in the plan and measure, measure, measure the results timely. Don't put the plan on the shelf, instead, refer to it often, tweak it when necessary, and acknowledge often the hard work that has been required to bring each success.

The next step is to compile and implement a business plan. While some of the data inside the business plan is directly related to the strategic plan, it should also contain more in-depth financial data and projections. Banking institutions often require a business plan with pro forma projections. Pro forma projections are a fancy way of presenting your data in a standardized, acceptable format and include most information required by banks.

You may use one of many methods to develop a business plan. There are a number of software programs available for purchase to assist you in the development of a business plan template. Business Plan Pro ® is a fairly common program. It is easy to use and is relatively inexpensive. Another is EZ Numbers® (www. eznumbers.com).

Another alternative is to seek help from an outside source to help facilitate the developmental process with you, such as SCORE (Service Corps of Retired Executives). SCORE works via the Small Business Administration (SBA) and offers free business plan templates with complete financial projections. To access this information, go to their website at www.sba.gov.

You may also consider hiring a professional consulting and/or training firm to help you. Companies like Waymaker Learning Corporation help both established dealerships and start-ups develop these plans. With years of experience in the field, our team of facilitators helps you zero in on the important targets needed to be successful. When using a firm like Waymaker Learning Corporation, you also get follow-on consulting and coaching to make sure the process stays on track.

Calculating the numbers to use in the pro forma is an exercise in accounting combined with your best "guesstimate." You should forecast as you plan it to be. Be careful about being overly optimistic with your pro forma projections as you want your plan to be considered well thought out and accurate.

For example, you should consider what your costs would be to operate each year for three years. Your estimates should be based on research and past experience (if you have any). Here are a few considerations when formulating your pro forma projections:
1) Potential expenses;
2) Potential income sources (unit sales, income from your service department, POS products, credit card income, interest income, late fees, repossession fees, etc.);

3) Estimate the tax rates for anticipated income level of your business; and

4) Be familiar with the industry and know the average expense numbers for buying, selling, and reconditioning cars, trucks, equipment, trailers, etc.

The data included in the pro forma projections should be reflected in a spreadsheet format suitable for measuring progress and results.

In conclusion, the strategic plan and your business plan must be integral to your everyday activity. If they are seen as something additional, then in most cases they are not driving your organization toward your vision. Instead, you will likely be doing work, but not always in sync with where you say you want to go. This approach creates false starts, sidetracks plans and far too often leads to failed businesses.

The late Dr. Stephen Covey, author of *Seven Habits of Highly Effective People*, wrote in this best-selling book, that we must first 'begin with the end in mind." Before we embark on a journey to nowhere, we must direct our efforts toward a goal and create a well-designed plan to get there.

There is one critical thing remaining and that is that you have to get started! Take action to team up with a coach, a mentor, a seasoned consultant or trusted friend, and design a strategic plan forward. Then start moving toward the vision you have for your dealership.

SPARE PARTS...NOTES

SPARE PARTS...NOTES

BIO: MARTY COATES
Co-founder and President,
Waymaker Learning Corporation

Marty Coates is a trainer and consultant to independent automobile dealers across the country. He has trained more than 10,000 dealer participants in the past four years alone. He maintains a License Sales Representative card in North Carolina. His passion for helping dealers succeed drives him to travel more than 180 days a year on average.

He is President and Senior Consultant of Coates and Associates, Inc., a consulting, training and speaking firm he started in 1992. He has presented keynote speeches and conference training to groups in many foreign countries and all across the United States. Marty has led a number of companies during his twenty-six year career, to include serving as CEO of FirstChoice Healthcare, PC.

He is co-founder of Waymaker Learning Corporation. Marty produces and writes his online blog, "The Coates Perspective," where he discusses current business and social issues.

A graduate of North Carolina State University (NCSU), Marty has completed graduate level work in Business Administration at NCSU and Webster University. He has extensive leadership training from many military schools via his 15 plus year career as an officer in the United States Army, U.S. Army Reserves and Army National Guard. He is a decorated veteran of Operation Desert Storm where he was awarded a Bronze Star.

Marty is a co-author of two Amazon.com best-selling books namely, *Think and Grow Rich Today* and *Transform* (with Brian Tracy). He has authored or contributed to a number of other books to include, *The Waymaker Principles...Eight Keys to Living a Meaningful Life*, *Race to The Finish Line* and the national award-winning work entitled *Roadmap To Quality*.

Contact Information:
Marty Coates
Waymaker Learning Corporation

1082 Greenview Drive
Florence, South Carolina 29501

www.waymakerlearningcorp.com
843-229-3546

WAYMAKER
LEARNING
CORPORATION

CORPORATE TRAINING	CONSULTING	PUBLISHING
Strategic Planning	Business	Business
Management	Management	Self-Improvement
Organizational Development	Personnel	
Sales	Compliance	
Customer Service		
Marketing		

www.waymakerlearningcorp.com

843.229.3546

CHAPTER TWO
Lease Here Pay Here (LHPH)
Our Story, and How We Figured Out the 10 Keys to Success
By Chris Martin, CMD

Over the last twenty-two years, our Lease-Here Pay-Here business (similar to Buy-Here Pay-Here with a few documentation, regulatory and compliance differences) has experienced many hurdles. Thankfully, we have always been able to get over these hurdles and continue to grow our business. This has been accomplished with hard work, as well as, considerable help from other experienced dealers and professionals that have been willing to share their expertise and insight over the years. I am hopeful this chapter will assist you in conquering this business, and you can add it to your list of benefactors.

CAPITAL - The first challenge that you deal with in the LHPH industry (unless you have extremely deep pockets) is the capital issue. I have heard several different experts over the years state that you can "sell yourself right out of business" because of the large quantities of cash it takes to start a LHPH or BHPH business. When dad and I sat down to do the projections for his new start-up almost twenty-three years ago, we figured it would take an investment of close to $800,000 to get through the first three to five years. Keep in mind this was starting with monthly rent on our LHPH lot of less than $1,000, minimal inventory, and just dad and a commissioned salesperson as the only fulltime employees for the first couple of years. It took that long to build the portfolio to a point that the company could justify paying me a minimal salary so that I could leave the bank and start working long hours, but for a whole lot more fun! By the way, we didn't have an extra $800,000 sitting around to plow into our new venture, but with significant investment from some good friends/shareholders and a good local bank that believed in dad, we were able to get started.

As you all know, it is much harder today to get financing than it was twenty-years ago. But it certainly isn't impossible and your chances of approval are better than average if you have: 1) significant experience in the automobile and/or finance industries; 2) a solid business plan with at least two or three years of projections; 3) a minimum of 20% equity (could be your own capital or that of shareholders); 4) a solid long-term reputation in the community; and 5) it certainly doesn't hurt to have a positive long-term relationship with a financial institution that has an appetite for this kind of credit. I know this sounds difficult, but in today's credit climate without all or most of these items it will not be easy to get funding for a LHPH or BHPH business.

For example, a few years ago, our line of credit renewal for our warehouse line (line of credit used to finance our LHPH portfolio) was as stressful and difficult as I can ever remember. We did get everything finalized satisfactorily, but the bank required significantly more documentation and clarification from us than it has in over ten years. A few things that I am certain helped smooth out what could have otherwise been an extremely bumpy process were: 1) the fact that we have always been very open and honest with our banker (thankfully, he is the same with us); 2) we have worked hard to provide timely, clean, and clear financial statements (whatever it takes…this is a must for you and your banker); 3) we have a great accountant that has significant experience with LHPH and standard leasing companies; 4) our payments are always on time or early; and 5) we go out of our way to quickly resolve problems (whether our fault or the bank's).

I hope you can see from this chapter that we view our relationship with our bank as a partnership. Over the years, we have taken the time with our banker to explain in detail (it will take several meetings, lunches, emails, faxes, etc.) what we do and how we do it. We have found if your banker doesn't understand what you do or if they don't understand the financials, they can't explain it to the Loan Administration Officer, who in turn won't be able or willing to try and explain it to the Loan Committee.

PERSONNEL - After you have your capital in place, you will need to look at how you want to staff your LHPH business. If you are going to add LHPH to an existing used or new car operation, then you may not need to add much in the way of staff. But you must keep the following priorities in mind and make certain you have the individuals in place to handle the following tasks:

1) General Manager & Buyer - These positions are probably going to be handled by the owner until the business can justify adding these positions. As discussed later, you have to have the right inventory at the right price point and a solid understanding of the car and finance businesses.

2) Sales - It is important to fill this position with individuals that can easily transition from a LHPH customer to a traditional retail customer and treat both with respect and appreciation...not easy to find.

3) Documentation - This industry is extremely regulated and you must identify someone that will "dot all the i's and cross all the t's", as well as, stay up-to-date on all the various compliance issues.

4) Titlework - This piece of the process may also be handled by your documentation person, but it has to be accurate and you must know which forms to use for each type of transaction (cash sale/lease/wholesale/sale with outside financing/etc.).

5) Payment Clerk - Are you going to appoint a certain individual or individuals to take payments as they come in? Don't let convenience get in the way of keeping solid controls in place to protect yourself from fraud and theft.

6) Bookkeeper - Either find a qualified bookkeeper (probably part-time), or your accountant may provide this service at a reasonable cost.

7) Collector (payments & insurance) - That's right, you are going to be collecting lease payments AND following up to make certain your lessees have the proper insurance coverage for the entire term of the lease. This is because you will be leasing a vehicle you own to another entity, and in the event of an accident, you could have exposure. Again, this is a vital position and should be handled by someone that can be firm and clear while maintaining a positive relationship with your customers (another easy hire, right?).

8) Reconditioning - You have to determine at what level you are going to recondition your vehicles, and then determine if you have the expertise and experience required to do this in-house or outsource it. It is a completely separate business and you better understand it before choosing to hire technicians and detailers versus outsourcing.

INVENTORY - Once you have the capital and personnel in place, you need to stock your lot with inventory. And I am like the rest of you-running from one auction to another, calling wholesalers, looking online, working other dealers for trades, etc. This has become a game changer for most of us. We are constantly looking for new ways to find inventory that works within our individual business model. I try to stock vehicles with Actual Cash Value's (ACV's) around $5,500. As you are all aware, this has not been easy, unless you want to pay $7,000 to $8,000 for it. However, one strategy that has worked extremely well for us over the last several years has been to explore every opportunity to network with other dealers and auction professionals. These relationships generate opportunities to purchase inventory for us almost every day. My involvement in our state and national associations has been vital in this arena. There have been numerous occasions at a convention, a seminar, or a meeting when another dealer or industry professional has offered me an opportunity to generate our kind of inventory.

You must also make certain you are stocking your lot with inventory that will run for the entire term of the finance contract. Once the vehicle stops running, your customer is usually going to stop paying. On average, we spend in excess of $1,000 reconditioning our vehicles. We want to ensure the car is in excellent mechanical condition and will run the term of the contract. There is no way to make them new, but you want to invest a little up front to keep your customer on the road and his/her payments coming in, so you can buy more inventory and keep repeating the process. Of course, we do have vehicles that break down before the customer makes their final payment. Unfortunately, a lot of our customers will not maintain their vehicles at the manufacturer's recommended standards. So we find ourselves in situations where we must assist the customer with repairs so that they can and will continue to make their payments. This assistance can be as little as making repairs at our cost (wholesale) and as extensive as making goodwill repairs, at no cost to the customer, and every possibility in between. Every situation is different, and you will need to gather the facts and make the best business decision for you and your customer.

Don't let personalities and emotions get in the way of making a sound business decision to keep your customer in his vehicle so he can continue to make his payment. If you don't help your customer to make the necessary repair; you will get the vehicle back; you will still end up fixing the vehicle; and the payments will have stopped. In the LHPH business, when the payments stop, you are done.

UNDERWRITING - Now that you have inventory, you are ready to start financing it for your customers. Once again, a fellow National Independent Automobile Dealers Association (NIADA) member taught me early on that proper underwriting is much more important than the amount of the customer's downpayment. Up until that point, I always thought a significant downpayment (20%+) cured all ills. Well, after a couple of conversations with that dealer at one of our annual conventions, I came straight back to the office and overhauled our entire underwriting process. I immediately cut our minimum downpayment in half, shortened our maximum term by 25%, reduced our average ACV by $1500, and actually began verifying income/employment and residence. These changes generated significant improvement in cash flow, repossession rates, and net profit; and reduced collection headaches significantly. Don't get me wrong, downpayment plays an important role with cash flow and a customer's commitment to the deal; but underwriting will likely determine whether your LHPH business is a short-lived failure or long-term success.

STRUCTURE AND DOCUMENTATION – First, are you going to be a lessor, a rental company, or a lienholder? There is a huge difference when it comes to the IRS and other state and federal regulators. However, it can be very difficult to see the difference when you are just beginning in this industry. This is one more reason to have a great attorney and accountant that understands this business, and to make certain you are involved in your state and national dealer associations.

You are a lessor if you are using the proper documentation (we will discuss in a moment) and you are structuring your leases appropriately. What I mean is, you not only have a Dealer Management System (DMS) that knows how to calculate leases properly, but you are inputting the appropriate information. The appropriate information would include: a reasonable lease rate factor that would not violate any usury laws in your particular state (keep in mind you must also have processes in place to ensure your pricing is not discriminatory); the appropriate state sales or highway use tax, and whether it is collected upfront or as part of the monthly payment; and, an appropriate and justifiable residual/purchase option. If the residual is less than 10% to 20% (but let your legal professionals be your guide) of the retail price of the vehicle at the time of delivery, then you may find that a regulator (IRS or some other three or four letter agency) will define your contracts as installment sales contracts masquerading as leases. This could be disastrous!! On an installment sales contract you are taxed on the entire profit on the sale of the vehicle in the year the vehicle is delivered, whether you realize (get paid by the debtor) any profit or not. If you have properly documented and structured your leases, then you will build your Leased Assets on your balance sheet and offset the Leasing Income as it is collected with the Depreciation Expense on your Leased Assets (again, a great accountant that understands this business is a must).

SERVICE CONTRACTS/WARRANTIES – Due to the substantial capital requirements we just discussed at the beginning of this chapter, we did not have the ability to finance service contracts in-house or offer a more extensive limited warranty on our vehicles the first several years we were in business. But we did see the advantage of these products to our customers and to our business. Most customers want the peace of mind, knowing they have coverage to protect them in the event of a major mechanical breakdown. We also recognized the potential for an additional profit center and the reduction of headaches when our customers had a mechanical breakdown. So when we started, we offered service contracts to our customers, but we did not offer to finance the service contract. The customer had to purchase it for cash, or we would write the service contract and the service contract provider would finance it (their pockets were a lot deeper than ours). Once we built up our cash flow/portfolio to a point that allowed us, we began marketing our service contracts and offered to finance them in the customer's lease. Another great option you need to consider as you build your portfolio and your business is to start a reinsurance company and use it to provide service contracts and/or warranties. The reinsurance model can be complicated and is covered in depth in another chapter. My only recommendation is to look at companies that have a positive relationship with your state and national dealer associations, and get several referrals from dealers that have used or are currently using this model.

PAYMENT ASSURANCE SYSTEMS - We have used payment assurance systems since before GPS was an affordable option-back when a basic starter interrupt system without GPS was the standard. As technology has improved and become less expensive, we have graduated to starter interrupt systems with GPS. This technology can make your business much more efficient. There are many different opinions on how to use this technology. We use them as payment assurance systems. What I mean is, we use these systems to assist us with collections and insurance, not just to locate and repossess the vehicle if a severe default occurs. We disclose and explain to our customers at delivery, the fact that we will use a "Payment Assurance System" to: 1) warn them of past due payments and insurance; 2) disable their starter if the default is not cured timely; and 3) locate their vehicle if recovery is required. Select a timeline for #'s 1, 2 and 3 that you think will work with your model and in your state. The key to making this process work as efficiently and as smoothly as possible is to limit the number of staff that can discuss payment arrangements with customers. You MUST stay consistent in your message with your customers in discussing your payment arrangement policy. If you make an exception to your policy this month, expect to make it every month (the customer will expect you to!). Starter Interrupt/GPS technology has also made it possible for us to reduce the number of collectors we employ and their corresponding salary expense. Of course, we have added the expense of the GPS units and their installation, but by using this technology, most of our customers call us to make payment arrangements instead of us having to try and run them down. If repossession is inevitable, we get the vehicle back sooner and with less recovery and reconditioning expense.

As far as installation and cost are concerned, it generally takes around 45 minutes for an experienced technician to install a unit and the cost of the units (currently $110 and up) vary depending on quality and features.

REPOSSESSIONS - Speaking of repossessions, I have learned some costly lessons over the years in this area, as well. Since I was a Field Representative (Collector) early on in my banking career, I figured when I went to work for myself I should be able to handle the recoveries myself. I found out quickly that professional recovery agents were much better at it than me and much more cost effective. A professional recovery agent should not only be great at locating and recovering your vehicles, but should be great at treating your customers with respect and capable of defusing potential problems in the field. I also demand that our recovery agents carry the proper insurance coverage to cover us in the event of an accident or the agent's negligence. No matter how good you feel about a recovery agent, always verify that they have proper repossession insurance coverage, not just "on the hook" coverage. Also, talk with their insurance agent and make certain that you will be notified if there is a cancellation, expiration or change to their policy. In order to get this protection, you must be listed as a Certificate Holder on the recovery agent's insurance policy.

The only thing better than a great recovery agent, is to do business in a state that allows you to report your vehicle stolen once a lease customer defaults and refuses to return your collateral. There are not many out there, but there are a few. Even if you operate in a state like North Carolina where you can't report a lease vehicle stolen when it goes into default, it is imperative to establish a positive relationship with the authorities in your market area. You will want your recovery agent to have a good relationship with authorities as well. For example, the recovery agent should immediately notify the proper authorities when they recover a vehicle. These relationships can pay huge dividends when you run into a situation where the officer on call is the difference between getting your collateral back and having a customer retain possession.

From time to time, you will have a lessee remove the starter interrupt/GPS unit. In the event this happens and you and/or your recovery agent can't locate your collateral, but you can locate your lessee- file "Claim and Delivery." This process requires you to hire an attorney in our market, but it is worth it if you are able to reduce the time necessary to recover your vehicle.

Once you have determined that recovery is necessary, every day that slips by costs you money. The customer or their friends are putting mileage on the vehicle, they are not maintaining the vehicle, they are wearing out tires/brakes/interior/etc., they are parking in tow away zones and getting the vehicle impounded (and you thought attorneys were expensive), they are getting into accidents and damaging or totaling your vehicle, etc., etc.,

etc. No question, good recovery agents and good attorneys are expensive, but the alternatives can be much more costly. So talk with dealers in your market for referrals and don't hesitate to contact your state or national dealer associations for referrals when you find yourself in an unfamiliar market. The laws and regulations can be dramatically different in other states.

INSURANCE - Of course, you are also going to need proper insurance coverage as a LHPH dealer. In addition to the normal Garage Liability, Dealer Bond, Errors and Omissions, etc. you will also need Contingent Liability Coverage to protect you in the event one of your lessees is in an accident without proper coverage. As I explained earlier in this chapter, the vehicle is titled to your company and you have exposure if the lessee has an accident without coverage or improper coverage.

Our company used a local insurance agent for many years before finally switching to an agent that specialized in coverage for car dealers. He was referred to us by the Carolinas Independent Automobile Dealers Association (CIADA). This is one of the best moves our company ever made. Prior to changing agents, we had coverage we didn't need and even more alarming was the fact that we didn't have some basic coverage that could have potentially cost us our business. Our new agent was an expert in providing coverage for our industry and he was glad to help educate us on the kind of coverage we needed. In addition, due to this change, we have saved tens of thousands of dollars over the years in premiums.

REGULATORY and COMPLIANCE - Lastly, establish a good relationship with your local Department of Motor Vehicles (DMV) inspector. If you have a reputation of always handling your documentation properly and your customers fairly, your inspector will likely treat you fairly when unforeseen issues arise. The LHPH industry is highly regulated, but you can stay up-to-date on documentation and compliance issues by attending the compliance and documentation education offered through your state and national associations.

SPARE PARTS...NOTES

BIO: CHRIS MARTIN
President/Owner
Team E-Z Auto

Chris Martin is President and Owner of Team E-Z Auto, located in Fayetteville, North Carolina. Team E-Z Auto operates as a Lease Here Pay Here dealership and has been in business for more than 22 years.

Chris started his professional career with Wachovia Bank. In 1995, after serving as a Personal Banker, Branch Manager and Corporate Banking Officer and holding the title of Assistant Vice President, he left Wachovia and joined his father at Team E-Z Auto.

He is a graduate of North Carolina State University with a Bachelor of Arts Degree in Business Management and Economics.

Chris was the first dealer in the Carolinas to receive the Certified Master Dealer designation and was the Carolinas' Quality Dealer of the Year for 2003-2004. He is a Past President of the CIADA and NIADA. He currently serves as Vice Chair of the Audit Committee for NIADA.

He resides in Pinehurst, North Carolina along with his wife Maria and their two daughters, Anabella and Marissa.

Contact Information:
Chris Martin, CMD
Team E-Z Auto
3900 Bragg Blvd.
Fayetteville, North Carolina 28303
(910) 868-3000

Team E-Z AUTO

ONE STOP

CERTIFIED Quality VEHICLE

& In-house Financing!

with approved credit

CHAPTER THREE
Choosing the Right DMS Software Product

By Barry "Chip" Cooper, Jr.

I grew up in a DMS environment. In 1971, my father pursued a second career outside of his actuarial duties at a life insurance company in Raleigh, NC. He contracted with local car dealerships by offering them software that he had developed to assist them in accurately computing and disclosing interest rates, finance charges, total of payments and the ability to incorporate credit life and disability premiums, among other charges within their deals. Computers, then, were limited in their abilities and terribly expensive. A WANG calculator, linked with an IBM selectric typewriter were capable of fully completing the numeric portion of any bank contract automatically with the push of a button; however, due to computing memory limitations, most all alphabetic information had to be manually typed in redundantly on every subsequent deal form needed.

In those early years, software was in its infant stages and more a matter of the extra income from computing 45 days to the first payment and a forms completion convenience for the dealer. Today, it is an absolutely critical, necessary component for every dealership (small or large) to both prosper and remain compliant with both state and Federal regulations. The question isn't whether or not you need DMS software in your dealership, but rather what you should look for when choosing the right DMS for your dealership. The company that my father pioneered 43 years ago and began as a second career, rapidly expanded and became his primary business and focus. It continues to grow and prosper to this day. We've serviced thousands of dealers and we continually update and expand the software in order to remain competitive and meet the ongoing needs of our dealers.

DMS defined: DMS is an acronym that stands for Dealership Management System, which refers to a comprehensive software solution that performs a variety of tasks for your dealership. Notably, DMS software should include basic functions such as: Prospect Management, Inventory Control, Deal Processing, Management Reporting, Accounting, Buy-Here-Pay-Here tracking, Website and Marketing feeds, integration to third party suppliers, Compliance tools, among other features you will need to consider that we will discuss in this chapter. There are many "**abilities**" that you should take into consideration when choosing a DMS software product. I've broken them down into 8 categories that we will discuss individually:

- **Functionability**
- **Usability**
- **Expandability**
- **Reliability**
- **Marketability**
- **Compliance Ability**
- **Serviceability**
- **Affordability**

Functionability: The old adage that "one size fits all" does not ring true in the DMS arena. Although every dealership may have a degree of fundamental requirements from any DMS product, I recommend that you outline specific functions you will require from each department within your dealership. Will you need parts and service software, or will your primary business model be car rental software? Whatever your endeavor, it is preferable to find a DMS provider that can accommodate all of YOUR needs for each department; however, you may find that certain vendors specialize in specific products, but lack others. It's not uncommon to run parallel sets of software packages such as DMS with a separate accounting or CRM program, just inquire with your potential DMS provider and determine whether they can interface with the specialized programs you elect to use. Within each function you outline, it will be important that information is shared between software modules. Redundant entry is a thing of the past. DMS software should eliminate the need for double entry, reducing error rates. Some dealers focus too much on the "bells and whistles" of DMS software, spend a small fortune, and only end up using about half of what the product has to offer. Others put too much emphasis on the low cost of the software as their determining factor, only to discover later that they are missing the features they really require. Here are some basic functions to consider and include when choosing your DMS provider:

- **Customer Relationship Management (CRM)** – CRM Defined: a system for marketing, managing, and measuring a company's interactions with its current prospects and future customers. Within any DMS software product, there should be an inherent CRM module that includes tools to assist management and your sales force with scheduling appointments and following-up with prospective buyers. Additionally, CRM should include tools that enable you to remain in touch with existing customers by allowing you to send them notifications that may include coupons for specials you may run such as oil changes, special sales events, etc. CRM should also include tools that help management track its return on investment (ROI) with advertising sources and employee performance. Be aware though, that CRM is merely a tool. When properly implemented, CRM can help you attain and retain more customers. Ultimately, its success or failure weighs largely on both you and your staff. It's a top down approach. Management must be on board and expect its sales team to utilize the system. Left unattended, CRM software quickly erodes into CRM "shelfware".

- **Inventory Control** – A basic function within any good DMS product is the ability to manage all vehicles (active and sold). It begins with a VIN decoder that should first, validate and authenticate the vehicle identification number for accuracy. Second, it should populate most all applicable fields on the screen with the exception of any undeterminable fields, such as the current odometer reading, cost, and retail asking price. The ability to produce an FTC Buyers Guide for your particular state is a fundamental requirement from your DMS vendor. You should consider a vendor who generates both the Buyers Guide and a window sticker complete with accessories, on plain white paper from your laser printer as opposed to using carbon style forms that require purchasing a separate dot matrix printer. Tracking repairs and on-going expenses for vehicles is a common sought after feature within Inventory Control. Integrations to third party inventory venues may be important to you, such as vehicle history reports, value guides, etc. Ask your provider what specific integrations they offer. Finally, most dealers want the ability to attach digital photographs of their vehicles within the DMS in order to forward over to websites and flyers.

- **Deal Processing** – The ability to process the deal paperwork for any deal type, whether it be a cash, wholesale, retail, buy-here-pay-here, lease-here-pay-here deal, or any other type of deal should be at the core of any DMS software. Based on what sales types you will be engaged in, be sure that your provider offers the necessary forms that will be required and accepted by Federal, state, and lenders alike. For the most part, both Federal and state forms are programmed just as they are provided by the respective entity without much modification by the end-user (except for Federal Privacy Notices, as an example, which should be customized). If you are going to be involved in outside financing, however, remember the golden rule: "He who has the gold, rules!" There are different publishers of Retail Installment Sales Contracts on the market, and your lender will most likely dictate the contract(s) that they will accept. Don't just assume your DMS software has THE correct plain paper contract for your lending institutions. If your DMS software provider doesn't support, or is unable to print the contract that the bank accepts, then you really can't consummate a deal on your DMS system. Traditionally, most deal documents were acquired by dealers through some entity in carbonless multi-copy formats that required a dot matrix printer in order to penetrate the multiple copies. Today, there has been a shift towards printing forms, in their entirety, using just plain white paper from the dealer's laser printer. The exception to this would be multi-part secure documents that vary from state to state. Laser Printers aren't created equally though. It will be important to purchase an automatic duplexing laser printer (one that prints both sides of a document on one sheet of paper). Be sure that your prospective software provider supports automatic duplexing printers as well; don't just assume they do.

- **Management Reporting** – Over the course of supplying software to dealers for many years, it became apparent that dealership management reports were an important key aspect of any DMS software that a dealer used to measure their success. While reports must contain detailed, relevant information in order to aid the dealer in making future business decisions, additionally they should contain the flexibility to be modified by the end user. An easy to use, customized reporting module will serve as an invaluable tool down the road. Consider reporting modules that offer the flexibility of sending the report to your screen, printer, or has the capacity of downloading into a spreadsheet and exporting format for maximum flexibility.

- **Buy-Here-Pay-Here / Lease-Here-Pay-Here** – If you are going to be active in the financing of your own vehicles, then a robust tracking software tool will be an essential component of any DMS provider's product. You'll have a few decisions to make on how you want to structure your deals and the tracking methods that will be used. Simple Interest or Pre-Computed? Most dealers choose Simple Interest, for a host of good reasons, but it will be imperative that your DMS software applies the payments in accordance with how the corresponding contract that you elect to use, outlines. Depending on the magnitude of in-house financing you choose to engage in, it might be beneficial to seek the advice of a competent accountant with direct experience in the car business and in the field of establishing a Related Finance Company (RFC) in order to discuss ways to defer possible tax consequences for your dealership. For purposes of our discussion, if you envision a large Buy-Here-Pay-Here portfolio down the road, then ask your potential DMS provider if their software supports a Related Finance Company. Lately, there has been a trend by some dealers to engage in in-house leasing or renting of vehicles. While the laws for leasing or renting vehicles varies by state, generally speaking, there are tax advantages to leasing/renting in-house as well as differences on how repossessions are handled. Lease-Here-Pay-Here should be a discussion between you and a trained professional to see if the business model is for you. Ask your prospective DMS provider if they can accommodate in-house leasing or rental.

- **Accounting** – Some form of dealership accounting can be offered and included by DMS providers. Others offer integrations into third party accounting suppliers, like QuickBooks® by Intuit, and others. A discussion between you and your accountant in order to determine which option is right for you is warranted. Your accountant may have a specific program that he or she is familiar with and encourages you to use. If that is the case, then check to see if the DMS company supports an interface into the package your accountant recommends.

Usability: DMS usability is best described as how easily you and your employees can navigate the software product. At the core of any DMS, should be a simple, easy to use, intuitive interface that is consistent throughout the program. When evaluating DMS, it's generally a good idea to involve your employees, when possible, during certain aspects of the evaluation/demonstration period. They can contribute to the decision making process by offering suggestions and potential shortcomings of any software product as it pertains to their own experiences and responsibilities within the DMS product. After all, your employees serve in the proverbial trenches, day in and day out. If they aren't impressed with the ease of use, or the product lacks features specific to their own tasks then you can expect complaints from them down the road and lackluster results.

Expandability: Never say "never". I can generally classify independent dealers into two categories: Those that are into Buy-Here-Pay-Here, and those that are thinking about getting into Buy-Here-Pay-Here. Countless times I've heard from dealers that say, "I'll never get into Buy-Here-Pay-Here" and ultimately end up calling us wanting to know what steps they need to take in our software to begin tracking buy-here-pay-here customers. The wholesaler, who says he's only going to wholesale cars and will never need a retail license occasionally inquires asking what additional forms they need in order to start selling retail. Successful dealers may ultimately venture out into multiple locations. If you envision yourself aggressively pursuing this, then inquire whether your DMS provider can provide a solution for this by supporting a centralized database that is accessible and shared by multiple locations, yet still uniquely distinguishable by each lot location.

Flexibility: should be a forethought, not an afterthought between you and your DMS provider. Your initial business plan can change due to a host of reasons, economic and otherwise. Consider all of the features DMS software offers, envision future possibilities and avoid compartmentalizing yourself. Ensure that your DMS provider can meet your future endeavors.

Reliability: The platform that a DMS software package operates on generally comes down to a choice between a desktop version or a cloud-based version. While both can accomplish the job, there are a series of trade-offs based on which format you elect to use. A desktop version generally offers a degree of reliability that a cloud-based system cannot. We've all experienced internet outages at the most inopportune time. An Internet outage at your home can be frustrating, but it will cripple a cloud-based DMS software package when the outage occurs at your dealership during normal business hours. On the other hand, it's hard to imagine in this day and age, not taking advantage of the technology that the internet brings to the table. A good, stable DMS software package, in my opinion, is one that is functional with or without the Internet, yet utilizes the Internet extensively for software updates, offers remote data backups, OFAC checks, remote software access, marketing feeds and other aspects inherent in a web-based system. Uniquely classified as a "crossover" or hybrid edition of DMS software, offers you ultimate flexibility and the best of both worlds. Most all of us use some form of high speed Internet, but if your dealership resides in a location where access to the Internet is slow or even non existent, then a cloud-based system will be equally slow. A desktop version however will operate at a consistent speed irrespective of your Internet service provider. Data storage and data control is another consideration. If you are on a cloud-based DMS, then your software should automatically be backed up for you. For those that don't relish the idea of their customer information being housed "somewhere" on the Internet, a desktop version should offer you a variety of choices. You should be able to back it up locally at your location, configure it to optionally backup data to the Internet, or both. Ultimately, your dealership data is just that ... it's yours to control. Ask your potential provider what access you will have to your data if you discontinue their services, cease to exist, or have a dispute. Is your data readily available to you, or will you be forced to pay a subscription in order to access it?

Marketability: Statistically, over 80% of all car buyers now use the Internet to research vehicles prior to making a purchase. Keeping your dealership open 24/7 is a key marketing strategy in order to offer and sell vehicles to customers you otherwise would not have the opportunity to sell. While Internet marketing and advertising is covered more extensively in another chapter, you should ensure that you DMS software provider can offer you either a template or custom website design that is integrated within the DMS software. Vehicle inventory should originate from within the DMS software package and be made available to other venues including your website and others. If not, you'll be faced with the daunting task of entering (and deleting) vehicles multiple times, once in the DMS, again on your website, and potentially other marketing websites as well. From smart phones, to tablets, the world has gone mobile. Your DMS provider should offer a mobile rendition of your website for viewing on a smart phone. Additionally, your provider should offer integrated inventory data feeds to third party advertisers (both fee-based and free) and social media outlets as well in order to maximize your marketing potential.

Compliance Ability: Increasingly, your dealership is under constant scrutiny from both Federal and state regulatory agencies to comply with existing and newly passed legislation.

The penalties for non-compliance can be substantial. The agencies a dealer must comply with resembles a bowl of alphabet soup: OFAC SDN, IRS 8300, FTC, DMV Regulation Z, Regulation M, and the newest oversight comes from the CFPB (Consumer Financial Protection Bureau) in Washington D.C. Your DMS software should be able to perform some basic tasks, including the ability to instantly check your customer against the OFAC SDN (Office of Foreign Assets Specially Designated Nationals) list in order to ensure you're not selling to anyone on this government watch list (which at last check was over 900 pages long of fine print and updated weekly). Additionally, your DMS software should be tracking cash collected in a single transaction or collected over the course of a year. If the cash exceeds $10,000.00 in either scenario (and there are more scenarios), then your DMS should alert you to electronically produce an IRS Form 8300 and send a corresponding notification to your customer. Ensure that your DMS supplier has the tools available to help you comply with Red Flag Rules (combating identity theft). The FTC publishes the AS-IS Buyer's Guide in multiple languages and Implied Warranty formats, which are to be posted on the motor vehicle before presenting it up for sale. Your DMS provider should readily have this form available in multiple formats depending on the state you occupy. It's difficult for me to understand how a dealer can comply with some of these regulations without the aid of a DMS software product, or why they would even try without it.

Serviceability: You should give consideration to the time zone in which your DMS provider is located in relation to your dealership. What are their hours of operation? A dealer on the east coast, for example, who experiences problems and needs assistance from their provider in the early morning hours can find it frustrating when trying to contact DMS support staff that is located on the west coast, only to discover they won't be open for 3 more hours. In a worse case, you may leave a message for them at 9:00 am, (your time); only to discover that they called you back around noon while you were away for lunch. You, in turn, call back support around 1:00 pm, (your time) and attempt to resolve an issue that plagued you much earlier that morning. It will be important that your provider be accessible during YOUR business hours. Does the provider offer after hour and weekend support? Ensure that your DMS provider offers remote access support whereby they can remotely log into your computer and share your screen. This can be especially beneficial for diagnosing and solving problems, urgent downloads, or remote training for new employees.

Affordability: There are a variety of pricing structures that DMS Software providers charge. Some require long-term contracts and upfront deposits while others offer simply month-to-month subscriptions. I'm a big proponent of the latter. Month-to-month subscriptions ensure that your provider earns their keep each month. Don't hesitate to ask your prospective DMS provider to supply you with some references with which you can speak. The DMS software of the future is rapidly unfolding before our very eyes. From mobile applications, to digital signature pads, it never ceases to amaze me what technology continually brings to the table.
As I look forward, compliance is and will continue to be, a centerpiece of any DMS product. As features and benefits continue to expand in our industry, unlike motor vehicles, DMS software constantly remains affordable.

I still remember those early years, when my father demonstrated that WANG calculator with software he had developed and the IBM selectric typewriter. As a kid, I was amazed to see a typewriter that would, at a touch of a button, take off on its on and begin to accurately fill in most all of the spaces of a retail installment sales contract. Much like the player piano that was programmed to play a song, as well as any artist, unattended …

it was magical! Today, DMS has evolved into a serious tool that a dealer can't afford not to have. Continually challenge your DMS provider on what they offer you and where they plan to take you into the future.

SPARE PARTS...NOTES

BIO: BARRY "CHIP" COOPER, JR.
President
Commercial Software, Inc. (ComSoft)

Chip is a second generation President of ComSoft; a family owned and operated dealership management software provider located in Raleigh, NC. Chip grew up in an F&I atmosphere. The car business was standard dinnertime conversation. He has over 35 years experience in the automobile software arena. He works in conjunction with several state independent automobile dealer associations by assisting dealers in the classroom on how to efficiently and profitably operate as well as promote their dealership. He offers solutions to dealers in order to help keep them compliant with both State and Federal regulations.

Chip spearheaded the effort to make the Virginia Independent Automobile Dealers Association (VIADA) copyrighted forms available to dealers in an electronic format for their laser printer utilizing the ComSoft DMS product. Currently, ComSoft is the sole DMS provider that offers the optional use of the Carolinas Independent Automobile Dealers Association (CIADA) copyrighted forms in an electronic format from the dealers' laser printer. Chip continues to reach out to other state associations in order to facilitate their proprietary forms to the dealer's laser printer via the ComSoft program. The cooperative joint venture between ComSoft and independent automobile dealers associations across the country helps to ensure that associations continue to market and sell their forms without the necessity of the traditional, but aging, dot matrix printer.

Chip was born in North Carolina and has been a native of the state his entire life. He graduated Apex High School in 1981 and subsequently attended Western Carolina University from 1981-1985, during which time he interned with ComSoft. Immediately following college, Chip took on full time employment with ComSoft taking on the responsibilities of both building and servicing computers and dot matrix printers. Later, migrating to sales and support, learning every facet of the business prior to becoming Vice President and then assuming his current role as President.

Outside of ComSoft, Chip currently serves on the Executive Committee of the Sons of the American Legion. He is also a member of the American Legion Riders, volunteering in most any capacity that helps to serve both our active and retired military.

Contact Information:
Chip Cooper
ComSoft
Raleigh, NC
www.comsoft.com
919-851-2010 (work)

ComSoft

Dealership Management & Marketing Software Solutions

CHAPTER FOUR
Web-Based Technology Helps Today's Savvy Dealer Save Time and Money

By: Michael Samaan

I can honestly say, I wish I'd known then, what I know now, when it comes to the benefits of technology in effectively managing a dealership. I was in the dark, not realizing the tools available to me via a simple internet connection and computer terminal. Although a growing number of tools available to a dealer are just a click away, many dealers still struggle with business transactions.

When I first started in the car business working my grandfather's used car lot in South Daytona Beach, I was under the misconception that a customer would simply walk onto your lot, test drive a vehicle you both agreed was best for them, pay you the fair price you were asking, and ride off happily into the sunset. Oh yes, and then send you all of their friends and neighbors who needed a vehicle. As seasoned dealers know, that's not how it works at all. In fact, I am convinced that running a successful car dealership will turn even the most naïve individual into a cunning entrepreneur. After all, the car business encompasses wholesale, retail, financing, compliance, insurance, inventory control, marketing, rental, and in many cases, parts, service and body shop repair. Not to mention the most important component, money management. Make no mistake, as an independent dealer you will wear all of these hats, usually in the same day. You need as many resources as possible to help you save time and money, and web-based technology in today's industry can play a big part in your success.

Is Your Inventory Really Worth What You've Invested?

Obviously the most important component to selling a car is the car itself. You can build your inventory by purchasing a vehicle at auction, buying through the newspaper or internet, and of course, taking a customer's current vehicle in on trade. And here's the scary part – each one of these presents opportunities for fraud and a loss of big money to you.

Here is an example of what happened to me, I'm embarrassed to say, more than once:

A customer came into my Dodge dealership in rural Georgia and picked out a brand new 2007 Dodge Ram off the front line. The customer presented us with a 2004 Chevy Colorado to trade with 40,000 miles. We appraised the vehicle for $8500 (the Actual Cash Value (ACV) investment in the truck). The customer informed us that he still owed a payoff of $3800 to a credit union. No problem! I wrote the deal putting $8500 ACV into the trade and entering their payoff of $3800 at the bottom of the buyers order. As the payments were agreed to and the deal began taking shape, we called the customer's credit union confirming the 10 day payoff as well as their mailing address to send the payoff check. Everything looked good! I stood waving as the customer jumped in his new truck and drove off. We made a decent $2500 gross profit. Not a bad transaction right? Wrong.

A few weeks went by and we still had not received the clear title from the credit union even after mailing them a payoff check based on the initial confirmation of a $3,800 balance. We contacted the credit union to verify they had received the payment. They did and had satisfied their lien, but then forwarded the title to the second lien holder – a quick loan operation two towns over. Apparently, our happy customer had secured a $2,000 loan six months prior, had a $1,300 balance owed, and failed to share that information with us. Weighing the cost of a lawsuit to recover the balance against the potential recovery, we did what many dealers will do. We paid off the truck to get a clean title and cut our profit in half.

Here's the moral to the story. Had we looked deeper into the vehicle's history we would have most likely found the second lien holder and saved ourselves a lot of money and grief. While this isn't a scenario that happens at dealerships every day, the potential is always there and one misstep can cost you thousands of dollars.

Real-time Data Saves Real Money!

Today, dealers have access to technology that offers a cost effective solution to preventing fraud and ensuring smart decisions. Real-time web-based access to current motor vehicle records from multiple state databases through a company like Auto Data Direct is just a click away. These records are governed by the Drivers Privacy Protection Act (DPPA) and are only available to certain industries. Dealers are allowed to access and view the records, in most cases, under the permissible use of verifying information submitted by an individual to help prevent fraud (like the example of my Georgia customer). In most states the DPPA records contain the name of the title owners and registrants along with their current address information, general information on the vehicle, and any current interested lienholders who may have a perfected lien on the vehicle. This information includes the lienholders' address information as well as date of lien. Through ADD's DMV123 service, dealers can instantly access over 30 state databases for this critically important information. This quick and easy step in your sales process will save you time and most certainly money.

Is That Vehicle Hiding a Secret?

I do a lot of traveling and watch a lot of newscasts around the country. It's amazing to me how many local floods there are, not to mention the larger named storms that cause mass property and vehicle damage. Often these vehicles are shipped to auction across the country, or offered online, to be sold sight-unseen. Flood vehicles often are moved out of states where the damage occurred because some states make it easier to re-title a car that has been written off as a total loss, a process known as title washing. Those cars can end up with a clean bill of health, with no indication they were declared a loss in an earlier life. Tens of thousands of these vehicles were shipped to other states after being flooded in New York and other southern states following Super Storm Sandy, and unfortunately, this still happens today.

The National Motor Vehicle Title Information System (NMVTIS) maintains vehicle information by VIN, which aids in searching these discrepancies and alerts you that there is likely a problem. In addition to obvious problems like "Flood" title brands, NMVTIS reports provide the current and historical states of title, letting you know if a vehicle was recently titled in a flood-damaged area.

NMVTIS vehicle histories, also available through ADD, are a great cost-effective data resource online when buying a car for inventory or appraising a vehicle for trade. While maybe not as widely known as the other privately branded national history reports, NMVTIS is owned by the Department of Justice (DOJ), managed by the American Association of Motor Vehicle Administrators (AAMVA) and is a federally mandated consumer protection program. Everyday dealers are discovering this information tool that pools total loss, salvage and titling data from multiple state DMV's. Most jurisdictions update NMVTIS information either in real-time or nightly so the information is as up-to date as possible. As of June 2014 NMVTIS contains 96% of all U.S. DMV data. NMVTIS access is available to dealers online without minimum purchase requirements, contracts, monthly or annual fees. In most cases, you simply pay per pull. I am a fan of pay-as-you-go, because in many cases your lot traffic and inventory will vary depending on the time of year so you want to avoid being locked into buying a set number of reports under a strict timeframe. If you use a Dealer Management System (DMS), often NMVTIS will be available through your system provider.

In July of 2012, a California state law went into effect requiring that any dealer who offers a vehicle for retail sale in that state must obtain a NMVTIS report and have it available for a customer to view. In some states, a total loss vehicle brought in from another state with a title either in the insurance company's name or endorsed over to the insurance company, even if the title is "clean," will be considered a salvage vehicle. Used car dealers should take this into consideration when making purchases of wrecked or damaged vehicles being sold through salvage auctions with "clean" titles. If the seller of the wrecked or damaged vehicle is listed as an insurance company, the chances are very good that the "clean" title advertised is either in the insurance company's name or has been endorsed over to the insurance company as the result of a total loss payout. This means that neither the purchasing dealer nor the consumer will be able to get a clean title on the vehicle. A simple check of the vehicle in NMVTIS may reveal that an insurance company and/ or auction have reported the vehicle as a total loss or salvage designation, allowing dealers to avoid title headaches that may come with such a purchase.

Combine Real-Time Records & NMVTIS to Track Down a Vehicle

Dealers who act as lienholders or operate buy-here pay-here operations and related finance companies can use both real-time owner lienholder information, as well as, NMVTIS to their advantage. Quite frequently the owner of a vehicle that you have a secured interest in will relocate to another state. Under normal circumstances, you will be contacted of the move so you can re-record your lien in that state. Or, depending on the state, you won't be notified at all and the customer will just move and you'll be left without a new address. Sometimes, again depending on the state, it may be easy for the customer to obtain a new registration and title without your lien being attached.

Your customer can move two states over to a jurisdiction that does an inspection on the vehicle and simply asks your customer for their registration and if he currently has a lien on the vehicle. The customer tells the DMV there are no liens on the vehicle (sometimes the older the vehicle the less likely anyone is to research the history). The individual pays his/her fees and is issued a new title and registration, minus your recorded lien. A few weeks go by, you haven't heard from your customer and worst yet, he has missed the last two payments. You call the references and find out he has moved, but no one is willing to tell you where. If you have access to NMVTIS, you can enter the VIN and the NMVTIS report will return the title data history. You notice that two weeks prior there was a title change and new odometer reading in another state. You can then go to the DPPA real-time motor vehicle record search for the last state of title and find the name of your customer, the correct vehicle information, as well as their new address.

Of course, many times everything is done correctly on the customer's part, but you are just not properly notified that your lien was recorded on the new record. Many states do not offer an easy way to check and verify liens on motor vehicle records, so again, the web-based access will make tracking that vehicle much easier.

Electronic Registration Benefits Dealers, Law Enforcement and Consumers

Another web-based technology assistance tool that is gaining more and more popularity from state to state are online Print-on-Demand temporary license plates and Electronic Vehicle Registration services. There are many positive reasons for states to move towards electronic registration services whether temporary or permanent, not the least of which are the benefits to law enforcement. When a highway patrol officer pulls over a vehicle in a state without an electronic registration service they are flying blind as to who is in the vehicle and if the vehicle should be in that person's possession or not. Often times without an electronic registration system your customer is the last known registrant or the dealer. Then you could be contacted by law enforcement if there is any question around who should be in possession of the car.

The dealer definitely benefits from web-based electronic title and registration services. First, there is a psychological impact to the customer who sees you print the temporary plate and report to the state that their name and drivers license is now associated with that vehicle. Personally, I think it helps to reduce the buyer's remorse factor and you're less likely to have a car you sold the night before parked in front of your store with the keys shoved into the night drop box. From a compliance standpoint, having a running electronic manifest of your registration transactions makes state audits easy. Most systems provide you with an electronic log book to help prove your transactions were done properly. Many garage liability insurance providers also report that having the electronic report of the registration transaction is enough to prove that a car was no longer in your possession should it end up in an accident before the state receives your permanent registration paperwork. But this does vary by state law.

In many cases, the state allows vendors to provide space on the tag for the dealer to advertise or at the very least add their phone number or company email address. Remember that one of the best places to advertise your dealership is on the car you just sold!

Electronic Lien and Title Helps Protect Your Investment

One of the newest web-based services that is being legislated from state to state is the Electronic Lien and Title System (ELT). For dealers, ELT primarily affects anyone placing a lien on a vehicle, vessel or mobile home. If you are a buy-here pay-here dealer, or own a related finance company, the ELT service will become an integral part of your lien management process. However, if you do not or are not planning on financing vehicles in house please do not count yourself out of ELT. It has been my experience that many dealers, from time to time, will place a lien on a vehicle and hold paper for small amounts of money, so in this case you would still need to obtain an ELT number. Also, it is important to know the ELT rules of your state. Even though you may never place a lien, you will still be handling electronic lien titles when you trade in a vehicle. In some states you can choose just to leave the title and transfer it to the new owner without obtaining a new title.

If you are new to the car business, understanding how ELT works may require a quick explanation. After you file your lien with your DMV office or tax collector and hand over the paper title (or if the title is currently electronic, in some cases you will just turn in the appropriate lien transfer form), your lien and title now become electronic. A message is passed from the DMV to you through the state certified vendor of your choosing. Access to your lien records is available through the vendor's password protected web portal. All of your liens will be displayed while they remain here until an action is required. In most states you can either electronically satisfy the lien when the vehicle is paid off, choose to order a paper title through the system with your lien attached, or choose to order a paper title with the lien satisfied (actions do slightly vary from state to state).

Now that you have a general understanding of how ELT works, let's look at the benefits. Growing up in the car business many of my friends and family were, and still are, buy-here pay-here dealers. I can relate to the initial reluctance lenders have when the state takes their paper titles away. After all, that's your nest egg. I knew dealers who actually carried their titles around with them in a satchel and would put them next to their bed at night. When I was still in high school one of my mentors was one of the largest volume buy-here pay-here dealers in Central Florida. One of his biggest concerns at the time was fraudulent titles. There were and still are criminals who can get you a new title free of any liens, which can then be taken to a title pawn or small loan company as collateral. Many times the owner stops paying the original lienholder as well as the second lienholder and then it's a fight to see who gets the repo first. Essentially, an electronic system such as ELT puts a stop to this scenario. With the record housed electronically along with all the pertinent information from the title and registration record, loan companies can easily tell if a vehicle is already liened. And, titles cannot be recreated without the electronic lien being satisfied. The system won't allow it to happen, thus protecting your investment.

Another benefit to using ELT is the reduction in lost or stolen titles. Lenders who choose to use ELT, maintaining the title as electronic until either a payoff, repossession, or out of state sale are performed, are all but immune from this very common occurrence.

ELT was originally created to help the states save money on print titles, as well as, help enforce the data in their lienholder databases. However, the benefits to the individual lenders are great, and despite new system implementation quirks, the feedback from lender customers has been very positive. And again, the use of this web-based lien management process has proven to save the lender time and money.

Power in Numbers Through Your Association

Being a dealer today is a challenging endeavor with the high costs of inventory, insurance, and compliance activities, but it's worth it! The car business can be very rewarding and provide you with a great living. Most of the best operators I know are involved with their state and national associations. Many laws are proposed every year at the state and federal level that can drastically impact your business. The dealer associations provide their industry a collective voice working with vendor partners to help keep dealers in business. The minimal cost of annual membership goes a long way in supporting this effort.

SPARE PARTS...NOTES

BIO: MICHAEL SAMAAN
Dealer Services Manager
Auto Data Direct, Inc.

Michael Samaan's passion for cars has fueled his life-long career in the automobile industry. Michael began as a dealer wholesaling from auction to auction and selling cars from his family's independent auto dealership in Daytona Beach, Florida while still in high school. After starting college at Stetson University in Deland, FL, his interests turned to the franchise side of the business and he began working for the local BMW Mazda Volkswagen dealership in Daytona Beach, buying and selling their used vehicle inventory and learning the leasing, financing and new vehicle retail side of the business. He later moved to a manufacturer-owned Ford franchise in Palm Coast, FL and served as its used car manager, and later as sales manager. Working in franchise dealerships allowed him to receive several years of manufacturer and industry sales and service training which had afforded him the opportunity to become a dealer principal. He purchased his first new vehicle franchise in South Georgia and after attending the Daimler Chrysler Dealer Academy in Auburn Hills, MI, he continued to gain experience with management of six franchise lines, two used car dealerships, and a rental operation with locations in four cities.

He joined Auto Data Direct, Inc., (ADD) in 2009 as Dealer Services Manager and works with thousands of dealers nationwide to provide a suite of web-based tools aimed at improving their business efficiency in a cost-effective manner. Michael works closely with both State and National Dealer Associations and believes strongly in promoting the importance of dealer association membership and industry education. ADD's wide range of services for automobile dealers includes electronic temporary registration (temporary tags) in Florida, electronic lien and title services nationally, real-time access to motor vehicle registration and title information in 30 states, and access to the National Motor Vehicle Information and Title System (NMVTIS.)

Michael, his wife Christine, and daughter Sarah live in Tallahassee, Florida, where ADD is headquartered.

Contact Information:
Michael Samaan
Auto Data Direct, Inc.
1379 Cross Creek Cir.
Tallahassee, Florida 32301
Phone: 850-877-8804
Email: msamaan@add123.com

In today's competitive marketplace, independent dealers need every edge they can get. Speed and access to the right information can make all the difference at the finish line.

Auto Data Direct (ADD) offers dealers a single-source, web-based solution to work smarter, faster, and more efficiently. ADD's dealer tools put real-time data, paperless lien processing, low-cost vehicle history reports and more right at your fingertips, giving you that competitive edge.

Take advantage of ADD's great dealer tools and services:

- Electronic Lien and Title (ELT) Services
- DMV123 Real-Time Owner and Lienholder Search
- National Motor Vehicle Title Information System (NMVTIS) vehicle history reports
- Dealer Management System (DMS) integration
- Federal Total Loss/Salvage Vehicle Reporting

Visit ADD123.com and see why thousands of dealers use ADD's time- and cost-saving services.

Use promo code CIADA14 at sign up and receive free account activation!

AutoDataDirect, Inc.

1.866.923.3123

CHAPTER FIVE

Handshake to Handshake...
The Auto Sales Process

By: Rod A. Heasley

As I have been blessed with the opportunity to travel this great nation in the last 18 years offering sales and motivational seminars to the independent automotive industry, I have been struck by the absence of knowledge and education on the fundamental basics of having a successful, simple process to sell and deliver a vehicle.

If you are reading this book because you are a brand new independent auto dealer and are looking for a daily guide to follow, or you are an auto dealer veteran looking for ways to improve your current operation, never lose site of the fact that being a student of the basics and having a sales process that you and your team buy into100% of the time will always reward you with benefits and success.

You must completely understand that true and rewarding success in our business of vehicle sales as an independent owner, begins and ends with your ability to be a leader. The sales process strategy, Handshake to Handshake, when properly applied, is a street proven basic auto sales technique that will deliver you to the end of the race with the positive outcome of delivering that vehicle to your new customer/friend. You will cross the finish line as the WINNER!

A simple, basic and positive sales strategy that allows you to turn a "no" into a "yes" and does not insult the intelligence of your customer, but in the end makes them your friend, will always stand the test of time. It always has and it always will!

Never forget that your customers are looking for Relationships not Transactions!

HANDSHAKE TO HANDSHAKE (9 STEPS TO AUTO SALES SUCCESS)
1. Meeting & Greeting
2. Building Rapport
3. Qualifying
4. Presentation & Demo
5. Building mental ownership
6. Price negotiating
7. Closing & Write up
8. Delivery
9. Follow up procedures

Three simple rules to remember throughout the entire 9 step procedure:

Rule # 1 – NO SHORTCUTS
Skip a step or two and you lose the sale.

Rule # 2 - SPEED KILLS
Slow down. Finish each step with the customer's approval before moving to the next one.

Rule # 3 - CONTROL
This one word directly affects your success in the auto sales process.

1. Meeting and Greeting
This is your ONLY opportunity to make a first impression on your potential new customer/friend. All the factors come into play here with regards to that "first impression" i.e. your

dress, your haircut, your body language, your speech, your attitude, and your handshake. Reversing the table here, stop and think about the last sales person you met. If you had a "negative "reaction to any of the above listed categories, then what was your first impression of him/her? You need to have a standardized greeting for your customers that give them warm fuzzies because you do not get a second chance to make a great first impression. The key to your approach is that EVERY customer gets treated like a family member. Within the first thirty seconds, you should have given a warm welcome including a firm handshake with one hand and delivery of your business card with the other. You want them carrying your card around during the entire presentation. Do not wait until they are leaving to hand them your card as it will probably end up on the ground.

2. Building Rapport

This stage is where you slow down (do not jump right into your sale presentation….not at this stage…..SPEED KILLS!). You must make the customer your friend by helping him relax and by establishing a relationship moving forward based on trust and confidence. Always remember to be friendly, positive, businesslike and enthusiastic. To be a top earner in this business, you must learn to slow the customer down and establish credibility. You must at this stage create the desire to buy from YOU! Find out where they live, how long they have been in the area, what they do for a living, where they go to church, what are their hobbies, etc. Do they belong to any civic organizations, where did they go on vacation this year, do they know any friends or relatives that have purchased from you, etc. The more you can engage them in a conversation about personal issues, the greater your chance of winning them over. Remember to direct your conversation to anything that slows them down and gives you the opportunity to lay the foundation for building a relationship. Do not yet, under any circumstance, talk about anything having to do with buying a vehicle!

3. Qualifying

Your ability to become an expert on qualifying a customer is where you will be setting the stage for more sales and higher profits.

During this conversation session, discreetly weave in the questions you need answered. For instance:

• What type of vehicle is the customer looking for? Why?
• What type of use is planned for the vehicle (business or personal)?
• Financing or paying cash? Monthly payment range?
• Trade or no trade? (What are they driving now?)
• What other dealerships has the customer been to and how were they treated there?
• What have you liked and disliked about your car buying experience so far. This will dictate to you the remainder of your presentation. Emphasis should be on what they like and you should stay away from what they do not like. Explain why you are different.

Here is the world's shortest selling course, always in this order and not open for discussion:
A. Sell Yourself
B. Sell your dealership
C. Sell your product

If they do not like you, if they have heard negative things about the reputation of the dealership, then the price and the negotiating is irrelevant at this point.

Remember at this stage they may have other priorities that can ultimately affect their final decision on who is going to get their business. Believe it or not, not everyone is a shopper for price alone! Items such as economy, safety, comfort, location, service and even the attitude of the salesperson are also important. "Price alone never did and never will sell a vehicle."

YOU MUST ALWAYS SEPARATE THE SELLING OF THE
CAR FROM THE NEGOTIATING OF THE PRICE!

4. Presentation & Demo Drive; and

5.Building Mental Ownership

You can use step #4 as another opportunity to continue building
the relationship with the customer, as well as, weaving in some of
the qualifying questions that are discussed in step #3.

Your most important selling tool may be having a proper
demonstrating procedure at your dealership.

First important step is that you never ask a customer if they want
to take a demo! Excuse yourself by stating you will be right back.
Get the keys and a demo plate. Here is where you start to gain
control by issuing some commands like explaining to them that
you will drive first while physically explaining the benefits of this
particular vehicle.

This is where you can start to get the customers excited as you
build the desire of ownership within the customer's mind. It is
here also that you can start to reposition their thinking on how
much they can really afford to spend on a vehicle.

It is imperative that you have a "planned "demo route already
established. You will always drive first on the way out to a
designated turn around point. This turn around point should
be secluded with no distractions. Your route should contain
some of the normal driving conditions that your customer will
experience in their daily driving routines, such as, entrance
onto a freeway, climbing hills, crossing railroad tracks, and even
navigating bumpy old roads.

You will be able to talk, as well as, ask more qualifying questions on the way to your turnaround point. Pull in and always turn the car around to point in the direction of the dealership.

At this point, you have arrived at a fantastic place to show the features and benefits of the vehicle while being away from any distractions on the lot. You will have your customer's undivided attention.

Take advantage of this situation by opening the hood of the vehicle to display and explain the type of engine in the unit. Based upon the answers you got during your qualifying questions, you must explain why this engine meets their wants and needs. If you are really good you might produce a print out from the internet that shows highlights of this particular used vehicle. Again, this adds credibility to what you are showing and explaining to them.

Allow them to see the size of the trunk, as well as, the exterior features of this unit. You can have them stand back and study the vehicle, as you are away from all the other units and the confusion that normally happens at the dealership.

When you make statements about the particular vehicle they are looking at, remember not to assume that they know and understand what you are talking about, for example:

"Well folks, this car has a 2.0L Eco-Boost I-4 engine!"

Wow... that's impressive, but does the customer know what 2.0 means or what the L stands for? Do they know and understand what an eco boost is and how it benefits them, as well as, the I-4 part?

You must show the feature and then explain the feature to the customer. Next, tell them the benefit to them in their personal situation. Finally, do not insult their intelligence. Allow them to agree or disagree on whether or not a feature is important to them.

After your walk around presentation, turn and hand the keys to the one you have determined as the major decision maker. If possible, allow each decision maker involved to take a turn driving the vehicle. It is important by now that you have determined the main decision maker and have that person drive first. If you have more than one customer with you, always remember that you are to be in the back seat on the way back to the dealership.

While you are in the back seat, do not say a word unless the customers ask you a question. My philosophy here is that you are creating a mental post card of ownership. With the decision makers in the front seat, you want them to envision that they are driving down the road just as if they owned the vehicle. When this happens they will not want you in the back seat chirping away!

On the ride back, become a great listener because it is a time to be watching and listening for buying statements from your customers, for example, "Honey, what do you think the neighbors will say when we pull in the driveway with another red car?" or "Honey, Billy and Sandy will love this sound system when we go to the beach next week."

Hold that thought here! What did your customers just tell you in a roundabout way? Give up? They just told you that they are going to buy this car! How can that be? You have not negotiated the price yet. Thus the point of separating the selling of the car from the negotiating of the price! If they have thrown up any objections at this point, and you have not confronted and overcome those objections then:

YOU HAVE NOT SOLD THE CAR!

So here is the question of the decade, "Why would you continue pushing onward into the negotiating stage of the process if the unit is not sold?" You need to slow down and address each and every objection and get the customers agreement on these issues before you talk price!

One thing to remember at this stage, before you enter into price negotiating, is that by following all the noted steps up to this point and not taking any shortcuts, you have significantly increased your ability to get the customer back at a later point if they do not buy today.

Needless to say, by using this method for each and every customer, you will significantly turn more of your first time buyers into new customers!

Last, but not least, this process allows you to hit all the major objectives that I mentioned previously, such as establishing a relationship based on trust and confidence, as well as, allowing you to maintain control of the selling situation!

6. Price negotiating; and
7. Closing & Write up

If you have followed my procedure step-by-step to this point, then I can make the statement that every customer will end up here, closing the deal, and actively involved in price negotiating! First of all, let's be sure that your desk is clean and organized and professional looking (rather than looking like a flea market table) and that you have at your fingertips all the tools you may need to close the sale. All the things on your desk can be a distraction, as well as, an escape for your customer when you want their undivided attention.

At this point, make absolutely certain that you do not take any phone calls. If you are alone, then let it ring to message because NOTHING is more important at this time than the potential sale you have directly in front of you.

The following is the sales procedure I recommend you use at your dealership as you enter the most crucial stage of the sale:

A. Tell the customer that you would like to document and review some of the details and issues you have already discussed. Take out a blank piece of paper or worksheet and start reviewing important topics about the vehicle they are looking at, allowing you to not only slow the customer down, but take time to build value in the vehicle.

B. If there is a vehicle to be traded in, take the time to appraise the vehicle; but if someone else is doing this then you should have the appraisal with you when you sit down. You should also, at this point, cover the positives and negatives of the trade. Get the customer to agree with the findings of the appraiser with regards to miles, condition, and obvious repairs that will be needed to re-sale the car. (If you are in a state that has state inspection as a requirement, always be sure to check the expiration date of the current inspection sticker on the car. If it is up in a month a two, you might be looking at a huge repair bill in order to get a new inspection).

C. Next, you want to list the selling or asking price of the vehicle, as well as, show the trade value. Calculate the price difference, immediately followed by the number of months and the monthly payment price. (You must do this all in one breath with no hesitation then SHUT UP. It is very important here that you maintain direct eye contact with the decision maker. Remember in negotiations the first one to speak loses!)

D. At this point, the customer will declare what kind of buyer he is by what he objects to the most in regards to the numbers you just gave him. There are six kinds of buyers:
1. Full Gross
2. Re-conditioning
3. Trade allowance
4. Difference
5. Payments
6. Discount

After you determine the kind of buyer you have, zero in on that objection and overcome it. Remember that no matter what the customer's objection is, you never argue his point. Keep the negotiating process from being confrontational. (Do not forget that the customer's comments are what start the negotiating process).

E. I want you to envision that you have the customer in an empty house and each of his objections is an open window in the house. With each objection that you overcome, you are closing another open window in the house. If there is one objection that you do not overcome, that will be the open window that he jumps out of and you lose him! If all doors and windows are closed and locked, then you win and can proceed to write up the buyers order.

Take a deep breath here and CONGRATULATIONS!
You just accomplished your most important daily objective …
YOU JUST SOLD A VEHICLE!
(But, the job is not done!)

8. Delivery Procedure

In my opinion, points #8 & #9, are the two most important steps of the entire procedure. Each of these steps and the procedure you choose to follow will have a direct effect on your future success in this business!

The first thing you want to do is remember the feelings and emotions that you experienced when you bought a new vehicle for yourself.

In most cases, the customer is making the second largest purchase, next to a house, that they will ever make in their lives! Does your current delivery procedure reflect that type of situation?

My recommendation here is that you do what you must do at your location to make the delivery the "Golden Moment!" Here is a brief delivery checklist to guide you:

- Set a specific time and make sure you are there and prepared.
- Check all the paperwork for accuracy and completion, ahead of time.
- Inspect the car prior to your scheduled time and make sure it is RIGHT from bumper to bumper.
- Start out by explaining any warranties that may be in effect.
- Throughout this process, reassure the customer of his decision to buy this car from you and this dealership!
- Demonstrate how to operate all the extra features on this particular unit.
- Take the customer for a short delivery demo and make sure everything is as promised and always remember to thank him for his business.
- Ask for referrals!

Always consider the fact that this is the moment the customer will remember the most about the entire buying process. Do something special that the customer will be sure to share with all his friends. Do not just ho-hum, sign him up and send him on his way. Remember, make it the "Golden Moment."

9. Follow up Procedures

Now that your "marriage" to the new customer is complete, it is time for the "honeymoon"- Follow up.

Most follow up systems require the salesperson to follow up owners periodically for no apparent or logical reasons. When the salesperson follows buyers in a helter skelter way, they eventually contact a buyer who is sore about a problem that needs attention, or possibly about some discourteous treatment. At this point, the salesperson gets "chewed out" for something that he had no control over. When this happens a couple of times, the salesperson no longer wants to conduct customer follow up.

Here are some brief steps for you to follow:
- Contact the customer three (3) days after delivery (by phone) asking if all his expectations on the vehicle have been met and if there is anything that you can do for him at this time?
- Continuously during the honeymoon stage, when contacting your customer/new friend, ask for referrals to his friends, neighbors, coworkers, etc.
- Third Contact- Ten days after delivery of the vehicle, mail a handwritten "Thank You" card, and again, ask for referrals.
- Every birthday and or anniversary, send a handwritten card to the owner and his immediate family. You should do this as long as he drives your car. Think about this procedure- for a family of four, it is at least four emotional, meaningful, contacts a year. If he drives your car for three years, that's 12 impressive contacts from you personally and/or your dealership.

Most auto salespeople fail to realize that one of the great secrets of car sales success lies in a salesperson's ability to follow the same successful procedures, day-after-day, week-after-week, month-after-month, and year-after-year.

In my opinion, successful salespeople are the ones who persist,

persist, and persist. To many car people, this is extremely difficult and boring. Unsuccessful people in the car business are the ones who continually jump from one project to another, because in reality, they get bored doing what it takes to become successful!

You should develop and work with a program that is designed to help you retain at least 90% of your buyers. In my opinion, you must become personally and emotionally involved with the buyers. In other words, know what is important to them and contact them after the sale using a methodical procedure.

Let me conclude here by asking a few questions. If you religiously use my follow up techniques,

- From whom do you suppose the customer is going to buy his/her next car?
- Who do you suppose is going to get his/her service business?
- Won't he/she feel guilty just driving by another car dealership?
- How much money does this follow-up program cost you?
  The Answer is $0. And finally,
- How can you afford not to have a consistent, written, follow-up system at your dealership?

If you keep the customers to whom you have already sold happy, they will continuously be out there working for you! They are your security blanket for future success in our business!

CONCLUSION

In this chapter, I have attempted to offer a brief, non-drill down, detailed description of my Nine Steps to a Successful Sales Procedure.

To be a top earner and performer in our business, as well as, a true professional, you and your team must always be aware of what you are doing and exactly where you are in each and every step of my procedure.

Check and re-check your procedures on every attempt with a customer to know exactly where you are in my process in order to get the sale and the best possible gross.

Always use poise in your approach. Enthusiasm and confidence must be portrayed in every sales attempt at your dealership. Boldness and persistence in asking for and expecting to sell that car NOW should always be at the top of your mind.

In my 37+ years of being involved with automotive sales, I have never met a natural born salesman who will succeed in the industry on that trait alone. They all need a map, guide, or Bible to follow on a daily basis and they all need to be trained continuously!

In my training sessions, I like to state the following formula that I have personally comprised:

Time + Error = Experience
Experience = Knowledge & Enthusiasm
Knowledge & Enthusiasm = Sales and Profits!

I could never stress enough that you and your employees instill the above formula into the everyday routines and procedures at your independent car dealership.

The fundamental basics to be successful in our business have never changed. Never ever forget, THERE IS NOTHING "AUTOMATIC " IN SELLING A VEHICLE !

SPARE PARTS...NOTES

BIO: ROD HEASLEY
President and CRO (Chief Relationships Officer)
KISS Concepts Group LLC

Rod Heasley is the President and CRO (Chief Relationships Officer) of KISS Concepts Group LLC a North Carolina based Independent Auto Dealer Services & Consulting agency. KISS Concepts Group has branch offices in Texas, Ohio, Michigan, Virginia and California.

Rod most recently served as Executive Vice-President of sales and marketing for Peritus Portfolio Services (PPS). PPS is a Texas based company that specializes in the purchasing of auto secured bankruptcy notes as well as bulk accounts receivables. He was responsible for training, certification and immediate supervision of Peritus's 123 business development managers nationwide. Rod has over 30 years in the automotive retail sales & ancillary products industry.

Mr. Heasley is a contributing international writer, and has had numerous articles published nationally, as well as in Canada. Heasley is a highly sought out speaker and presenter for national auto industry conferences .He regularly conducts sales training seminars and motivational workshops for NIADA state dealer associations and is the author of the 2014 National NIADA Best Practices dealer training series titled: "Street Level"- Bankruptcy 101, and "Regulation and Revenue...After the Sale". Rod has served on the executive board of directors, as well as an executive officer for several State Independent Dealer Associations.

His upcoming book entitled "**Back to Basics-Relationships not Transactions**" is a hands on simplistic guide to operating a successful independent auto dealership and is expected to be published in the first quarter of 2015.

Contact Information:
Rod Heasley
(Cell) - 248.880.7263
Email: kissconcepts@outlook.com

CHAPTER SIX
Why Reinsurance and "Doing the right things" go hand-in-hand

By Tim Byrd, Best-Selling Author

Our nation recently lay to rest an iconic figure, Maya Angelou. What an inspiration she was. One of my favorite quotes attributed to her is, "People will forget what you said, people will forget what you did, but people will never forget how you made them feel." This is so very true in life and especially in this career you have chosen. I recently had the great fortune of listening to two great speakers back-to-back at a conference in Las Vegas: Chuck Bonanno and Dave Anderson, both of whom are car business experts and trusted friends.

One thing that we three agree on as the most sound of business practices is to care for your customer. If you are reading this book, you are certainly in the car business and maybe in the Buy Here Pay Here business (BHPH). Please, if you don't make a concerted effort to always do the right thing by treating your customer with the utmost respect, please get out of the car business. You are stinking up the place.

For those still with me, here is some advice from a guy who has 25 plus years in this wonderful business and from the friends he listens to: Make a positive difference in your customer's life. As my mentor Zig Ziglar would say, "You can get everything in life you want, if you will just help enough other people get what they want." There are plenty of people who try and take advantage of their customer. In collection departments, I hear that around 18% to 20% are problem people. That means that nearly 80% are trying really hard, despite their hardships, to do the right thing.

There are things that you can do, differently than most, which will make a difference in the lives of your customers. Your customer is the most important part of your business. They are not an interruption; they are the purpose. What if you treated them that way? Remember, you provide transportation to a segment of our population that are predominantly low wage earners, whose lives depend on their car to get to work, school, church, etc... You, in turn, depend on their steady payments to stay in business.

I know, you're thinking, "Hey, I'm pretty good at what I'm doing." I want to help those who want to be GREAT! "The enemy of great is good!" so says my friend, Dave Anderson.

How do you become GREAT in this business? Dave Anderson says "Be Brilliant in the Basics." Chuck Bonanno says "Provide World Class Service." I say "Love your customers." These are three similar cornerstones to building a GREAT business.

"AS IS"

Many dealers take the "AS IS" approach to car sales. Was the car sold "AS IS" or as the salesman said, "We go over every car with a fine tooth comb, believe me, if you have a problem we'll take care of that." Sometimes a judge gets to decide.

I meet with dealers all the time who tell me they sell all their cars "AS IS". I have seen very expensive cars, $30,000 SUV's with "AS IS" marked on the Buyers Guide. Would you advise your mother to buy that? In most cases the dealers are so concerned that they are going to have to pay to fix something that they have opted for an "AS IS" policy on ALL their vehicles. There are dealers who just sell crap, which is why the Used Car Salesman ranks right up there with lawyers and politicians and we have a Consumer Financial Protection Bureau (CFPB) in the first place. The actions of a few reflect badly on us all.

There are many problems with the "AS IS" mentality, and my good friend, Jim Radogna, with the College of Automotive Management compliance consultants department, has outlined many of these pitfalls in his article Used Car Warranties: What You Don't Know CAN Hurt You. In his article, he talks about Expressed Warranties and Implied Warranties. Take heed. As he warns, "Now I'm all for dealers protecting themselves, but unfortunately, automotive law is not that simple and 'protecting yourself' can be far more challenging than just slapping an As-Is guide on the window."

Jim further states, "Rarely a day goes by without a dealer somewhere receiving a letter or lawsuit regarding an alleged breach of warranty."

The federal Magnuson-Moss Warranty Act, the Uniform Commercial Code (UCC) and various state laws (including used car Lemon Laws) all govern warranties on motor vehicles. Breach of warranty claims are extremely common and can lead to serious legal consequences for a dealer.

If you want to keep the CFPB, the FTC and other government watchdog and consumer protection agencies out of your business, I suggest you take care of your customer. I suggest you listen up.

Reinsurance Introduced

My expertise is in the reinsurance business. Why Reinsurance? It's what smart dealers do. It provides the tools necessary to help you be a great dealer, to keep your customer in reliable transportation, and to be the dealer that sells them their next TEN cars. Your customer may not remember the great features on their car or how much they paid, but what they will remember most is how you treated them!

Reinsurance helps you provide World Class Service without going broke doing it. In fact, you can improve your profit while doing it. Statistics show that one third of failed relationships with customers is over mechanical breakdown. They are sold a car, it breaks down, and they cannot afford to fix it. In case you are wondering, in most cases this is your fault as a dealer. If a BHPH customer financed their car with you for 24 months, serviced the car and made their payments, don't you think it should run for at least 24 months? Now, I am not naïve. Cars break, but don't you be naïve either. When the cars break, the payments are going to stop unless you fix their cars and get them back on the road! As Chuck says, "Customers don't pay for cars that don't run!"

Consider how much it costs to get a customer in the door the first time. Consider that payments are the lifeblood of the BHPH business. Then if your attitude is still "too bad so sad," your current system is costing you a fortune. I CAN FIX THAT! How? My answer can be your answer with reinsurance.

Reinsurance allows the car dealers to warranty their vehicles by establishing a nationwide mechanism, customer funded, which insures that there are always ample funds available to fix those vehicles; not a third party service contract, which costs you in the long run more than the repairs, but your OWN warranty company.
Why not have a system in place that no matter where your customer drives that vehicle, should they breakdown you have a plan and the money set aside to get them back on the road. The beautiful thing is that with reinsurance your <u>customer</u> continually and painlessly reserves for the unexpected breakdown. THEY are reserving for it.

For the BHPH dealer, your reinsurance company will provide premium finance for your customer's warranty; therefore, not requiring you to pay the full price of the warranty up front, which would deplete your lending pool.

A prorated portion of the cost of the warranty is collected from the customer's payment and forwarded to your reinsurance trust account. This will provide a constant stream of reserve to ensure that when problems arise there is a well-funded system in place. Problems are taken care of, your customers stay on the road and they continue making payments.

Selling Extended WARR Service Contracts

You may have talked about selling Extended Warranties. The Magnuson–Moss Warranty Act would begin by correcting you right here. You don't sell warranties. You sell Vehicle Service Contracts (VSC). Warranties come with the price of the car. Vehicle Service Contracts are sold above the price of the car and usually for additional profit.

This section is about selling Vehicle Service Contracts (VSC) and about improving customer relations through the sale of VSCs. Through the years, experience has proven that people who purchase VSCs are more likely to purchase their next vehicle from you, because should a problem arise, even out of town, it is taken care of. It is also evident that those same customers are more likely to have their service maintenance work performed at your repair facility. It just makes for happier customers and that relates to greater profits.

Vehicle Service Contract sales should be a task performed by the whole sales team, not just an after-thought by the salesperson or F&I manager. Management should make a point to encourage a three-step approach to VSC endorsement by the salesperson.

1. The first step towards a good VSC penetration is during the Features and Benefits presentation by the salesperson. As you complete your walk around and are going over the Federal Buyers Guide which indicates the warranty offered by the dealership say, "You will be glad to know that we offer very comprehensive extended parts and labor agreements to extend protection far beyond the vehicle's warranty period, for your added peace of mind. We will tell you more about that later on."

2. The second step is during the sales process. Ask "Does your trade have an extended parts and labor agreement on it?" Regardless of the customer's response "Yes, No, Maybe, I don't know" follow up with, "The reason I ask is that our used car buyer will usually pay a premium price for a trade that has one, because he knows that if there have been any problems with the car it has been fixed properly and timely." Just plant the seed, that's all.

3. The final step for the sales person is on the way to meet the Business Manager, say "I am going to introduce you to my manager. He/she is going to check over the figures and paperwork to make sure we have done everything properly. Be sure you ask about our extended parts and labor agreement. It's very important. Most of my customers take advantage of it, and all of my friends and family do. It has saved some of them a lot of money."

That's it. A three-step endorsement for the salesperson is all that is needed.

The three-step approach is designed to build value with the customer. It is important that the salesperson not try and sell the VSC to the customer. Customers resent two different presentations on the same product.

At this point, the salesperson has done his/her job. Now, it is up to the manager to build enough value that the customer justifies buying the VSC. It is always best to set the stage to provide testimony or evidence on how the VSC has benefited and saved others from the unwanted LARGE repair bill.

Some of the most successful VSC salespeople such as Josh, will have a worn out part on his desk to show the customer. Josh uses a fuel injector module. This part alone can cost at least $1800. He also provides a repair bill on the work performed on the fuel injection system. This particular part is especially effective because it is small, computerized and expensive. "It is hard for people to believe something you can hold in your hand can cost so much to repair," he says.

Remember, Vehicle Service Contracts can be the second highest source of income to a dealership, after the car sale itself.

Points to remember:

1. Stay consistent with price. If you discount, do so only with a good reason.
2. Go out and meet your customer at the beginning of the sales process. Bring information from your conversation back into your sales presentation.
3. Don't make your presentation at your customer. Make it for your customer. Get them to ask you questions.
4. Listen to understand, not to respond.
5. Relate a personal experience of a need for a vehicle service contract.
6. Remind the customer of the rising cost of parts and labor.
7. Offer a choice of two plans.
8. Always breakdown the cost of the plan to a monthly payment increase- dollars per year or cents per day.
9. Remind co-signers of the importance of making sure the car is protected.

Benefits of VSC:

1. Coverage is good anywhere in the United States or Canada.
2. Transferable should they decide to sell it.
3. Provides a pro-rated refund should they decide to trade the car in. They only pay for what they use.
4. No limit to the number of claims that can be made.
5. Increases resale value.
6. Pays out of state repairs with a credit card, avoiding the reimbursement hassle.
7. Provides a hedge against inflation. Using today's dollars for tomorrow's repairs.
8. Cost can be included in the monthly payments or carried on a credit card.
9. Protects customer against overpriced or unnecessary work.
10. Peace of mind for parents with college students.

Another great benefit of having a reinsurance company: YOUR Dealer-owned CPO Program!

Franchise dealers are rocking the world with CPO (Certified Pre-Owned) cars. The news reports that Certified Pre-Owned Sales Topped $2 Million for 2013 and the demand is RISING! Every subsequent quarter seems to surpass the previous quarter. AutoTrader.com reports that two thirds of all consumers begin their search looking for a Certified vehicle. The majority of used-car buyers intend to purchase a Certified vehicle. Statistically, those consumers admit they are willing to pay an average of $1380 more for a certified vehicle over a comparable non-certified vehicle.

Even though 65% of buyers start their search looking for a certified vehicle, only 1 out of 20 used cars sold are certified. The demand is MUCH greater than the supply. The industry NEEDS more certified cars, YOUR certified cars.

So why is there such a huge, ongoing demand? Many car buyers are looking for the best of both worlds, a reliable like-new car with a warranty at a used car price. The certified car meets that objective for an overwhelming number of buyers. Experts agree that this is not a fad, but a permanent and growing segment of used car sales.

Customers are drawn to Certified for the security of a pre-inspected, warranted car and for the simplicity of having their dealer pre-screen their car for hassle-free shopping. That peace of mind, for many consumers, is worth the added price of purchasing a Certified Pre-owned vehicle. As an added bonus, banks also substantiate the added value and will generally advance more for a certified vehicle.

So how much more is a certified vehicle worth? The premium price for certified vehicles vary widely depending on the vehicle's age and class. The facts show that consumers can pay over $3,000 more for the satisfaction of a certified vehicle. The industry average is over $2,000 and rising every year.

What if you only increased your gross by half the national average? Do you think that an extra $1,000 per car would make a difference in your bottom line? Many of those cars are already in your inventory.

We all know how important it is to turn your inventory. What if you could turn your inventory 40% faster? According to the automotive research firm, CNW, certified units stay in inventory an average of 25 days, compared to 41 days for the same age and model non-certified vehicle. We all know how important that is…40% more important.

You have to admit, these are some pretty compelling facts. So why isn't every dealer offering a certified program? As I mentioned first, most of the franchise guys are. Traditionally, certified programs are a factory or OEM sanctioned program for franchised dealers only. They are rocking. In December 2013, certified sales were up 9.4% over 2012. It is hard to compete with that, especially when you are unable to compete on a level playing field.

Many independent dealers know the value of certified and try to go it alone. That's a hard sale. Buying certified is synonymous with buying peace of mind. The customer's "peace of mind" needs something more than the backing of the dealership. Something more than an oval "Certified" sticker on the windshield like every car lot in the country. So do the lenders. A growing number of states, like California, now have or are considering statutes outlawing dealers from having an in-house, slap a sticker on the car, "Certified" program.

Unfortunately, most attempts to organize a certified program for the independent dealer have failed, even on a national level. Even with all the benefits listed above, these programs failed for many reasons:

1. A true lack of understanding of the independent market by the warranty companies, who send new car warranty salespeople out into the independent market to see how much they can make stick;
2. Sending out used car warranty salespeople, who are used to getting one or two warranty sales out of each account and truly don't know anything about the independent automobile business. Many independent stores have 30 different service contracts available and are loyal to none. If you go into their store, there is a rack of brochures that would rival the tourist brochure stand at the roadside rest stop;
3. As a result of #1 and #2, there are not enough warranty sales and warranty companies do not reserve enough because rates were established based on an expected large volume; and,

4. Finally, the death nail: claims exceeding reserve. This is all prompted by the fact that the dealer has no skin in the game. It becomes a cost of sale, an expense. So to offset the expense, some dealers file claims on everything that comes up, i.e. "recon" their cars. The warranty company, in an attempt to keep the Titanic afloat, appeases the dealers by paying what would otherwise be called good will. Claims exceed reserve, game over. The honest dealer is then left with a defunct program.

There is a better way. There is a national company who has 25+ years in the car business, a managing agency that is an expert not only in franchise and the independent car business, but also expert in Dealer Owned Reinsurance Companies. It's who they are. It's what they do. They have recognized the problem and have now provided a foolproof solution:

A Dealer-Owned Certified Program. This nationwide certified program, through reinsurance, is individually owned by each dealer. Turnkey…the managing agency sets up the entire program. You the dealer get the best of both worlds. You own the company, so what you provide as coverage on your vehicles is an actual warranty, not a service contract. The premium cost for your warranty is ceded into your trust account. Only YOUR premium goes into your account and only YOUR claims are paid out of that account. The great thing is that it doesn't need to be public knowledge that you own the company because the managing agency, along with their expert partners, take care of EVERYTHING: claims adjudication, accounting, training, ongoing support, etc. All you do is sell more cars. In addition, you can up-sell your own service contract and reap the underwriting profits on that as well.

Here's an example of how it would work: When you sell a service contract for let's say $1595 and your dealer cost is $995 your store makes an immediate $600 profit. Then you send the $995 in to your warranty company. Around $200 goes to overhead/admin cost (typical of any warranty company). The remainder, $795, goes into reserve. If you sell 20 per month you would reserve $15,900 per month or $190,800 in a year. Even if you have claims of 50%, you would have $397.50 per contract or $95,400 annually additional profit. In other words, the sale you used to make $600 profit on, you would now make $997.50. Now you know why your service contract company loves you so much. Add to that your certified warranties and you're looking at more like $150,000 in additional profit.

Recap: Selling more cars, turning your inventory faster, making more gross profit per car sold, making additional profit on the sales service contract AND making the customer smile…now that's doing the right thing!

Dealer-Owned Certified, finally a smart approach to CPO for independents.

DCC: A dream come true for BHPH Dealers

For you BHPH dealers, there is one more elephant in the room I can remove for you: Lapsed insurance!

There's another one to add to the stack. Lapsed Insurance notifications. Another customer has decided that having insurance is not a priority. Some you can't blame. The premium is higher than their car payment. You have hired a full-time person just to make those calls every day, and for what, to cover your butt, that's what. What if they total the car? They can't afford to pay for a car they no longer have, plus you lose them as a customer, not to mention the loss of the car itself. So, you call them up, "You agreed that you would keep insurance on this car. If you don't have your insurance reinstated right away we are going to have to repossess your vehicle." But wait, they are paying you like clockwork. PAYMENTS are the LIFEBLOOD of Buy Here Pay Here.

The dilemma is do you just overlook the fact that their insurance has lapsed? They're making their car payment. You need them to keep paying, but your collateral is unprotected. So, (this is logical) you pay someone to call them and threaten to repo them if they don't SPEND MONEY WITH SOMEONE ELSE! OR you take a chance. You let them ride, unprotected. You, by the way, are the unprotected one.

The problem begins when the customer allows their coverage to lapse, therefore putting into jeopardy the dealer or finance company's collateral. Industry research indicates that 50% of most BHPH books of business are uninsured. Customers put an average of $300 into insurance policies that they let lapse within 90 days, essentially throwing away that money. Many dealers have personnel assigned strictly for the purpose of making collection calls for the Insurance Companies who are reaping the financial gains off the dealer's man-hours.

Have you wondered if there isn't a better way?

What if you made a deal with your customers? "You pay a little extra each pay period to me, in return, if you total your car or it's stolen and not recovered, I will forgive your debt to me."

That is the definition of Debt Cancellation Coverage (DCC). You collect the premium with each car payment. You can make it a part of their monthly payment to you or a side note. Debt Cancellation Coverage is a solution to relieve the lapsed insurance problem and turn what once was an expensive, never-ending problem into a tremendous profit center. By capturing the money the customer would be spending with the insurance company and ceding it to your Dealer-owned Reinsurance Company, you profit instead of the insurance company.

DCC alleviates the need for you to require full coverage insurance. DCC puts you in control when there are claims. Instead of dealing with the insurance adjusters, you have a professional claims team looking out for your best interest. Nationwide, dealers who offer DCC avoid unprotected collateral on the road and the need to absorb uninsured losses.

Further, DCC makes it simple for you to enroll, right away, your current customer base and your new customers, at time of sale.

This is NOT Liability Insurance. The State requires liability. YOU only require your collateral to be covered. Since you require it and you make collection calls on it, doesn't it make sense for you to profit from it? Besides, an added benefit for the customer is that they can usually get DCC AND a VSC for less than they can buy insurance alone from that other guy.

The bottom lines
As you can now see, owning your own reinsurance company not only makes it easy to do the right things for your customer, it makes you Brilliant in the Basics. It keeps your customers coming back and that, my friends, is the bottom line you'll love to count on!

SPARE PARTS...NOTES

BIO: TIM BYRD
Founder/President
DealerRE, a Tim Byrd & Associates Company

DealerRE is a managing agency located in Gloucester, Virginia, with expertise in Dealer-Owned Reinsurance Companies, BHPH Operations and F&I Development.

The stepping stones that brought Mr. Byrd to his admirable credentials have family beginnings. Even as a youth, he participated in and witnessed his family's grocery business growing to be the largest in several surrounding Southern Mississippi counties. During an era that birthed the Supermarket, Tim was instilled with the old-fashioned traits of persistent hard work and operating by the golden rule. These core values became his persona throughout his tour in the U.S. Coast Guard and subsequent operation of multiple businesses.

Starting in the field of insurance with John Hancock Insurance Co., Mr. Byrd became intrigued with the industry of car sales, deciding to plant his talent in that industry. Over the next several years, his exceptional performance as an F&I Manager led the way for him to become a renowned trainer for other F&I Managers. Tim was armed with the unique combination of "degrees" in insurance, sales, F&I, and servant-leadership ethics.

This talent nearly dictated that he begin his own company, which, for 20 years now, has successfully enhanced scores of dealers' businesses. Today, Tim reports, "Our team's knowledge of every aspect of the car business, combined with our commanding knowledge of reinsurance, allows us to be a trusted source to guide dealers to greater profits, in a simple, secure and successful environment."

Tim has been featured many times in The Virginia Independent News, Special Finance Insider, Around the Commonwealth, DealerELITE.net, The BHPH Report and the Dealer Business Journal. Tim is a sought after speaker and co-author of the **#1 Best Selling book "Unfair Advantage"**.

The same passion for others' business success can be found in Tim's love for his family, including five beautiful children. Tim summarizes, "above all, my passion as a Christian man strives to reflect the values of my Lord and Savior Jesus Christ."

Contact Information:
DealerRE
7319 Martin St. Suite 4
Gloucester, VA 23061
(804) 824-9533
Website: DealerRE.com
2-minute Reinsurance overview Video: WhyReinsurance.com

CHAPTER SEVEN
Buying Cars As A Dealer
By Billy Threadgill, CMD

Buying cars for our dealership is one of my favorite things to do. I remember in the early years of our business being sent out on the road to purchase cars. As I was bidding at auction on a car that I liked or needed, my heart would pound away inside my chest. Whether it was from fear of bidding, making a mistake, or simply from the exhilaration of the auction process I still can't answer. Probably it was a combination of all the above reasons. Outside of dealing with the exhilaration factor of the buying process, I want to try and help educate you of a few basic principles of the purchase process.

One of the main venues of purchasing vehicles is the auto auction process. Being familiar with the National Auto Auction Association's (NAAA) policies and procedures for the buyer and seller is mandatory for you as a dealer. Whether you are buying or selling at the auction, this information is fundamental to you being a success or a failure. Knowing how to represent a car you are selling at auction or understanding the representation of a vehicle you are purchasing at auction will make you profitable or not.

There are several fundamentals that you need to have knowledge of before attending an auction. The first of these is the "light" system that is standardized by the NAAA. The light system is used to describe the conditions and disclosures related to the vehicle being sold. There are four "lights" which I will cover:

1. Green Light - "Ride and Drive" - The vehicles sold under the green light are vehicles that the seller has normally checked before the sale. The green light signals that the vehicle is guaranteed under the conditions outlined in the arbitration guidelines section, except for specific disclosures or announcements made prior to the sale.

2. Yellow Light - "Announcements" - This light is an indication to the buyer that the auction or selling representative has made announcements that qualify or clarify the condition or equipment and limit the arbitration of the vehicle. This light can be used in conjunction with other lights in its system.

3. Red Light - "As Is" – A vehicle sold under the red light will only qualify for arbitration under the rules outlined in the arbitration guidelines section. "As Is" dollar amount, model years, and mileage is subject to local auction policy.

4. Blue Light - "Title Attached, Title Absent, Title Unavailable" - This light is to advise the buyer that the title is not present at the auction at the time of sale. For auction policy regarding titles, please refer to the title arbitration policy. If title attached, title absent, or title unavailable is not announced, vehicle can be arbitrated for misrepresentation.

Next in the step is doing a pre-sale evaluation of the auction inventory you desire to purchase. Remember, you are the consumer on this side of the purchasing process and need to be as knowledgeable as possible about the vehicle before you walk in the lane to purchase it.

When doing a pre-sale evaluation, you should develop a condition report either on paper or mentally that you consistently go through before every purchase. This should be done on every vehicle whether purchased at auction or by any other venue. Remember - be nosy!

1. Vehicle history Reports: There are multiple entities that provide vehicle history reports. The four that are most noted for their information are National Insurance Crime Bureau (NICB.org), National Motor Vehicle Title Information System (NMVTIS), CarFax and Autocheck. Please note that Autocheck is the only one recognized by NAAA and its members. Also, there is another investigation that I like and that's to call the franchise dealer who sells the make of the car you are interested in and have him run a repair and warranty history on the vehicle in question. Don't forget the small things like checking to see if the oil filter on the car is a manufacturer's oil filter or an after-market oil filter. These are all indications of the type of maintenance the vehicle has received.

2. Mechanical Check: Before starting the vehicle, do a mechanical check. Always inspect the engine oil and levels, transmission fluid and levels, engine coolant and levels, and power steering fluid and levels. Any compromised fluid will throw up a huge red flag as far as the mechanical stability of the vehicle. Next, start the vehicle and listen for any audible sounds that are not normal in the operation of the vehicle. Also, check for exhaust noise, catalytic convertor presence and fluid leaks.

3. Frame and Body Repair Check: Look for consistent paint color on all panels and panel alignment at all connecting joints on the vehicle. Check for welds around the radiator support and front-end sheet metal components to see if the stamp welds have been replaced. Check all the bolt-on panels for replacement and/or paint lines from body repair/repaint. Look at front and rear bumpers to see if frame horns or frame rails have been damaged and/or repaired. Another possible indicator of previous body and/or frame damage is tire wear and tread wear.

4. Interior Evaluation: Check for wear on all the interior panels of the front and rear seats, door panels, headliner and all glass components. Also, while sitting in the vehicle, check all power options for operation since these can be very costly to replace. Check the brakes for safe operation before attempting to move the vehicle in any direction. Also, check rubber pads on brake pedals for wear or replacement. Upon starting the vehicle, you will need to check and make sure all the warning lights and systems operate as they should. If any warning lights remain lit after starting, this could result in a costly repair, which will eat up your profitability. If at all possible, take the vehicle for a test drive to check the engine performance, transmission for shifting and/or possible slippage, rear axle operation and noise, four-wheel drive front axle operation and noise, and transfer case operation and noise. While driving the vehicle, you can determine the stability of the front end and steering gear, etc., and operations of the front and rear brake systems. If your state has an inspection process that a car must pass before selling, now is a good time to check all these safety components for their functionality.

Surprisingly enough, you may want to determine whether this vehicle belonged to a smoker/non-smoker and whether the previous owners were pet owners, especially with cats and dogs. Many people have allergies and these factors may eventually matter.

The condition report that you develop should include a numeric-grading factor that you can take and apply methodically to help with the decision on what your purchase price of the vehicle should be. The refurbishment costs will play a critical role in the amount of money you can pay for the vehicle.

There are many ways to purchase vehicles on auction. Most of us like to see the car and enjoy the auction "buzz" or experience. The physical auction is the venue that I enjoy best. It's most interesting to see how hundreds of different dealers evaluate the vehicles they are purchasing. It is amazing how one day I can walk into the auction, develop a list of some 30-50 cars to purchase, and walk out with 10% or less of these vehicles. The next week I will attend the auction and have four-five cars to purchase and be able to purchase them all. I guess that's why they call it an auction!

The physical auction process normally has more finality to it than Internet auctions. The buyer can purchase, pay, transport, etc. all on the day of the auction, and it is finalized. The Internet buyer, on the other hand, can buy online, but must overnight or wire transfer payment to the auction and normally will have a week lag time before receiving his purchased vehicle.

Also, the physical auction pits one dealer against another dealer. This drives the price of the vehicle up and reduces profitability. I have seen some dealers bid on a vehicle just because they did not want another dealer to get it. These practices are not profitable for you or anyone else and are immature in character. I have also seen other dealers bid on cars that I bid on because they know how I pre-evaluate my list of cars; therefore, they use my pre-evaluation as their condition report.

The physical auction is especially relevant to dealers over the age of 55 due to their lack of computer skills and knowledge about simulcast sales. Internet auctions are becoming more widely used today than in years past. Can you purchase a vehicle online and be confident in your purchase? If a condition report with "integrity" exists on the vehicle that you are looking to purchase online then I surmise you can purchase that vehicle with confidence. If there is no condition report of a vehicle you are looking at online, I suggest you steer clear of that vehicle and find another one elsewhere. Most wholesale auto auctions have condition reports, or can do a condition report for you of a vehicle you are looking at online.

Reasons for purchasing online, in my opinion, include the ability to find vehicles not available in the dealer's geographic location and the integrity of the condition reports continue to improve with the online auction and its community.

If you purchase a vehicle online, always have a frame and mechanical post sale inspection done on the vehicles you have purchased. The best protection you have from buying a vehicle you will not be happy with is purchasing the post sale inspection. It also provides you with a vehicle in which you and your eventual customer can be confident.

You now have a good understanding of the auction policy and procedures that are standardized. At this point, let's discuss auction access. Auction access is the premiere dealer registration system of which I am aware. You simply fill out their registration packet and submit it for approval. Once it's approved, most auctions will simply allow you to get a bidder's number to purchase vehicles-either physically or online. You will be established with a dollar limit that you should monitor and not exceed. This is normally the limit of your floor plan, if you use one. A bank letter issued by your bank may also determine it. If you are a new dealer and have neither of these, they may approve you on a "cash only" basis to begin with. As your dealership grows, and you establish some financial history over time, this should be able to be changed.

At this point, you are becoming well equipped to attend the auction. You are familiar with the light system and have been approved through auction access for buying or selling. What's next? Hopefully, at this point you have formulated a business plan and put it in writing. Your business plan will help determine what you need to purchase to accomplish your objectives, and will help you in determining how much capital you will need to accomplish the objectives you have set forth.

There are two things that greatly influence the buying process for me. If I am buying a vehicle that I already have pre-sold, I look at market results for that particular vehicle, add to it the buyer's fees associated with the auction, if applicable, and then factor in the transportation costs associated with that purchase. Don't forget to include any refurbishing costs that may need to be done before the sale. Average industry reports estimate $700 per vehicle for refurbishment. Now that I have determined the actual cost of the vehicle, I can add my profit to the cost and give my customer a purchase price of the vehicle that they desire to purchase. If this is a quick sale, you may decide to take a smaller profit since your holding cost of that vehicle is greatly reduced.

When purchasing a vehicle for retail to fit my business plan, I have taken the time to know what cars will work for my business. If I am attending a physical auction, normally I prepare a vehicle listing and determine which vehicles I am interested in and develop that into my workbook. If these vehicles have a condition report generated by an auction this is a great help for me, but I do need to reaffirm the integrity of the condition report myself, if possible. Many of us still like to touch and see the unit we are trying to buy. Once you have checked the unit, I suggest you run your vehicle history reports that check the unit's previous history and check to see if the vehicle has any open recalls.

When we examine the used car supply and analyze it, used vehicles come from five basic sources of which I am aware. The first is the auction process that I have tried to explain in detail to the new dealer. While not being a total education, I hope it's a good start. Secondly, we will discuss buying a car from an individual. There are many pros and cons to buying from individuals. One pro is that many times the private party seller's vehicle can be purchased for less than the wholesale price at auction, and there are no fees associated with the purchase. Also, often you are purchasing a vehicle that has been well maintained during its previous history, possibly with maintenance and service records. And finally, most private party sellers are more interested in collecting the money for their former vehicle and may be interested in negotiations in their asking price.

As far as the cons of buying from an individual, there is always the challenge of meeting someone that you don't know at all. There are also no warranties associated with the private party purchase. You must do your due diligence on the vehicle by way of a vigorous and thorough test drive and pre-purchase inspection. Also, a must is to obtain history reports and check vehicle identification numbers to ensure there has been no tampering. Last, but not least, never pay a private party seller in full for his vehicle if he doesn't have a clear, unbranded title.

A third source of used cars is purchasing units from a franchise or independent dealer. This is a great way to purchase vehicles and even though you may have to purchase vehicles you don't want or need, you should be able to dispose of these and retain the one you want. Dealers normally package vehicles so they can dispose of the ones they don't need mixed with a few desirable pieces. In purchasing these units, remember to use the same method of what to pay and how much to pay. Use market reports and trade in values to support what you pay along with maintaining your profitability.
Fourthly, you may develop relationships with leasing or rental companies. Fifthly, there may even be wholesalers in your area. Many times wholesalers with whom you have developed relationships can get units to you that you individually cannot get done.

Many people use different sources of information to arrive at what they pay for a car. I don't endorse any particular one of them. National Automobile Dealers Association (NADA), Black Book, Kelley Blue Book, just to name a few, are reliable sources of information to use as a guide. I am a staunch believer in using market reporting to determine what I will and can pay for a vehicle. Manheim, Adesa, Servnet Auctions, and Auction Broadcasting Company all provide these market reports to keep us apprised of market values-almost on a daily basis.

In closing, please remember to never pay for any vehicle for which you do not have a clear, unbranded title. The one exception is to an auction that will give you a title guarantee document upon payment if they don't have the title on hand.

Hopefully the information provided will help you become a more proficient and profitable dealer in the years to come.

SPARE PARTS...NOTES

BIO: BILLY THREADGILL
Co-Owner, Van's Auto Sales
Senior Vice President, NIADA

Billy Threadgill has been a car guy his entire life. He grew up working part-time in a franchise store running parts, sweeping out the shop bays and other odd jobs. After graduation from high school, Billy attended Francis Marion University and then joined his father in his independent dealership, Van's Auto Sales, in Florence, South Carolina in 1975.

Today, he is principle owner of Van's Auto Sales and the local franchise of U-Save Auto Rental. His father and one of his sons work at the with Billy at the dealership.

Billy is a Certified Master Dealer (NIADA) with nearly 40 years in the business. He has served in leadership positions in the Carolinas Independent Automobile Dealers Association and the National Independent Automobile Dealers Association to include, CIADA President and Chairman. He currently serves as Senior Vice President of NIADA.

He along with his wife of 37 years, Dottie attend Florence Baptist Temple where he is active in numerous capacities. He has two sons, Chip and Michael, who are still very much a part of his daily life.

Contact Information:
Billy Threadgill
Van's Auto Sales
Florence, SC 29501
(t) 843-662-5631

Van's Auto Sales

A locally family owned Florence, SC used car dealership that offers quality pre-owned Cars, Trucks, and SUVs that will fit your budget. We offer BUY HERE PAY HERE on the lot financing, as well as in house BANK FINANCING with low rates!!

We serve the areas of Florence, Darlington, Marion, Dillon, Cheraw, and more!

Our staff can help you find the vehicle you are looking for.

CALL, CLICK, OR COME BY TODAY!

843-662-5631 | www.vansautosales.net

2801 E Palmetto St | Florence , SC 29506
Located one mile east of the Florence Airport.

CHAPTER EIGHT
How to Succeed in Buy Here Pay Here
By Russ Algood

Many dealers have had long-term success in the Buy Here Pay Here (BHPH) business. Most dealers have contemplated getting into the BHPH business, but wonder if it is right for them or if they can fund it. In this chapter, I will cover some of the major advantages and disadvantages of the BHPH business, and five keys to success in BHPH –Capital, Proper Inventory, Underwriting/Deal Structure, Collections, and Building a Customer Base.

The advantages are plentiful, starting with the fact that running a successful BHPH operation can be very profitable year after year. Secondly, once you have built your portfolio, payments on BHPH accounts provide a steady and predictable cash flow to help you weather the ups and downs of the car business. The BHPH dealer is not subject to the changing sub-prime credit market because the dealer controls his own financing. BHPH dealer profit margins on sales average up to 100%. Interest rates on the contracts typically are at or near state maximums averaging over 25% APR, providing the BHPH dealer with additional profit opportunities. However, most BHPH dealers view the high level of repeat and referral business as one of the biggest benefits of BHPH. This business is generated because the customers come back to your lot repeatedly to make payments and frequently have friends or family riding with them. Many customers come to think of the dealer as a friend they can trust.

The major disadvantage of the BHPH business is the capital requirement. A dealer self funding a BHPH operation will generally require a minimum of $500,000 and up to $2,000,000 of working capital. For this reason, most BHPH dealers use third parties to fund a portion of their operations, lowering their self funded working capital needs to as low as $100,000. Most BHPH customers are non-prime or sub-prime credit risks. Collections and repossessions are part of the business but when handled professionally are seldom, if ever, confrontational. Most BHPH dealers will use starter interrupt/GPS devices to improve collections and minimize credit losses. Some dealers, due to performance, staffing or compliance issues, will have third parties handle the collections and/or repossession activities. One important factor to minimize loss rates is keeping the vehicle in good working order, which will frequently require the dealer to assist with repairs after the sale until the contract is paid off.

Capital

Adequate capital is the most important aspect of becoming a successful BHPH dealer. If you run out of money before you reach the point of being cash flow positive, your chance of success is virtually non-existent. As they say, "it takes money to make money". It is important to note that a BHPH dealership is more of a financial business than an automotive business.

The capital needed for a BHPH operation will be substantial with an operation doing 10 BHPH deals a month requiring around $500,000 and 25 deals a month requiring $2,000,000. Actual capital requirements will vary based on the average price of your cars and the length of term on the contracts. There are three major areas requiring substantial capital for the BHPH dealer. First is the working capital needed to fund the daily operations of your dealership. The second is the cost of your inventory. The third and largest source is the capital required to fund your contract receivables. Only a few dealers are able to handle all of their capital needs without borrowed funds.

It is recommended you have sufficient working capital to cover 2-3 months of expenses, plus 25% of the cost of your vehicle inventory to cover cars that are not eligible for floorplan or on which you have made curtailment payments. Additional working capital requirements include parts, shop equipment, tools, DMS system, office furniture and contracts in transit. Working capital requirements will account for 12-20% of your total capital requirements.

Floorplans are lines of credit to finance your vehicle inventory. Floorplans will typically allow you to finance the full purchase price of vehicles purchased at auction. Some floorplans will also allow you to finance trade-in units or repossessions. Floorplans are short term financing which typically require monthly principle reductions, also known as curtailments, on each unit and full payoff on a unit if it remains on floor after around 4 months. Floorplan financing will account for 15-25% of your total capital requirements.

The most common means of funding contracts is with a finance company or a bank. Advance rates on BHPH contracts vary based on the underwriting standards, underlying collateral and the financial strength and credit of the borrower. Banks are typically lower cost, however, few banks loan to BHPH dealers and most of the banks that do will require you have well over $5,000,000 in contract receivables and a long track record of successful operations. In addition, banks will have a list of financial and performance covenants and frequently have lower advance rates than finance companies, requiring additional dealer investment. A finance company is often the best choice for BHPH dealers selling 75 or fewer BHPH deals per month. The past several years have seen a number of finance companies enter this space. Working with a company such as Ace Motor Acceptance Corp (AMAC) that provides both floorplan and contract funding is advantageous. When you use one company for floorplan and another to fund your contract receivables, you may be required to payoff the floorplan before you receive funding on the contract. This can significantly increase your working capital needs and thereby the amount of your own money needed to run your BHPH business. One big advantage of a company that provides both is you will be able to apply your funding amount to the floorplan on the sold vehicle, thus eliminating the additional working capital required when using separate sources. Whether you deal with a finance company or a bank, it is important to work with a company that understands and that is committed to the BHPH business. The Senior Management team at AMAC is composed of experienced veterans of the automotive and finance industry. It has collectively owned and operated multiple independent and franchise dealerships, successfully developed AMAC, and helped dealers throughout the southeast achieve success by tailor fitting programs to suit individual needs and goals. Contract funding will account for 65%-75% of your total capital needs.

Inventory

A dealer needs to understand his customer base in order to properly purchase vehicles for his lot. Consider the types of vehicles popular in your area. For example, if your client base is younger individuals in a metro area you will need to carry a higher mix of small and midsize cars. But, if you're in a rural area with lots of farming and construction work, you will need a higher mix of trucks. A dealer will also need to consider incomes in the area. The dealer needs to purchase inventory that will provide payments in line with the weekly income of the customers living within 5–10 miles of the dealership. For instance, if most of your customers can afford a $300 monthly ($75 weekly) payment you will need to target purchasing inventory for between $2,500 and $5,000. Whereas, if you are in an area where $400 ($100 weekly) customer payments are the norm, then you can target $4,000 to $6,000 vehicles.

Underwriting & Deal Structure

Underwriting is a key to the success of every BHPH dealer. Underwriting can be broken down into two categories, the customer and the deal structure. Always remember you don't make your profit until the customer pays you.

The Customer

In evaluating a customer, a dealer should always pull credit and review the past credit, which is generally very limited or derogatory. Many customers will have prior repossessions or bankruptcies. Pay close attention to prior auto credit. If a customer has several repossessions, all in the first year, you can expect that customer will not pay you either. If he/she paid for his/her last car your chances of repayment are much better. If the customer has had prior repossession(s) you should ask them about what caused the repossession so, if avoidable, you don't put them into the same situation. For example, if a reduction of income caused the last repossession because they could no longer afford that high of a payment, you would structure a deal with a payment they can afford now. Another example would be they travel to see relatives who live 750 miles away once a month, which doubles the average customers driving, so the car doesn't last the term of the contract. You would need to keep the term short on any contract with this customer. Prior addresses are another valuable piece of information, especially if there are addresses well outside of your area which could make both collections and repossession more difficult. Also look for recent addresses that are inconsistent with the credit application given by the customer, such as they list 5 years at their current address but have 4 different addresses showing in the bureau during that time. You should discuss these with the applicant.

There are several areas that every deal should be aware of when reviewing a customer's credit bureau. The first one is "Red Flag Rules" which identify potential identity theft with the applicant. Red Flag issues can consist of notifications and warnings from a credit reporting agency, suspicious documents, suspicious personal identifying information, suspicious account activity, or can come from other sources like a customer or a law enforcement authority. When the credit bureau shows a Red Flag alert you should get a copy of the customer's driver's license, proof of residence, and if the warning involves the social security number, then you should get a copy of their social security card. The second area to look at is Office of Foreign Asset Control (OFAC) warnings. An OFAC warning exists when the person on the credit bureau is considered to be a "person of interest" to the government. It is very important that all OFAC warnings are cleared before a car is sold to the applicant.

The Deal Structure

Providing a deal structure that works for both the dealership and the customer is another key factor to being successful as a BHPH dealership. The proper deal structure will be affordable for your customer, for a term no longer than the useful life of the vehicle, and provide the dealership solid profit margins.

To provide a deal structure that is affordable to most BHPH customers, a good rule of thumb is to keep the monthly payment less than one week's take home pay. You also need to review how much is paid for housing, and keep the payment plus their rent at no more than 2 weeks take home pay. If a customer has had a repossession in the past year, or while on their current job, keep their new payment at least $50 below the prior payment. If a customer can't afford the payment, you will likely end up with a repossession.

There is an old saying in the BHPH business, "When the car quits running - the customer quits paying." With that in mind, it is important to structure the financing so that the car will still be running at the end of the contract. To estimate the remaining useful life of the car, you will need to consider how many miles you expect the car to last based on it's current condition, make, model, age, and engine. Most customers will drive 15,000-20,000 miles a year, but some will drive substantially more. Someone driving 100 miles roundtrip to work each day will drive far more than someone who lives a mile or two from their job. How long the car will last will also depend on how much you are willing to do in repairs and maintenance to keep it running.

Down payment is another important factor in your underwriting decision. We recommend getting a minimum of 10% to 20% down plus taxes and tag. Down payments below $800-$1,000 often lead to what I call a renter's mentality. When the customer is tired of the car they quit paying and you get your "rental" back. While a large down payment does not guarantee a customer will pay, it does lower your risk and improve your cash flow.

Dealers use varying strategies related to dealer markup. Some dealers target $2500-$3000 profit margins while others target $4000-$5000. Lower profit margins allow for shorter contract terms and put the customer in an equity position sooner, which allows you to sell them a car up to a year earlier. Typical profit margins in the industry are 40%- 50% of selling price, which means selling the car for around double its wholesale value. This level of mark-up, combined with proper underwriting, deal structure and effective collections will lead to success in the BHPH business.

Collections

Now that vehicles are being sold, the dealer must collect. The collections process begins when you close the deal and deliver the car. Dealership personnel involved in closing the deal and delivering the car should be trained to explain your expectations for repayment-payments are due on or before the due date. The dealer needs to disclose the use of a starter interrupt/GPS device; most vendors have sample forms for this disclosure. The customer needs to be informed that if for any reason a payment will not be made by the due date, they need to contact you with the reason why and when they will be making the payment, and that failure to do so may result in the car not starting. When customers understand this they are much more likely to pay on time and to contact you ahead of time.

In most small BHPH dealerships, the owner or a family member handles collections. However, as a dealer's BHPH business grows, it will become necessary for him to hire designated collections personnel. They will need to be properly trained on effective collection techniques that treat your customer with respect, as well as, collection laws and regulations. The dealer should plan to have one full time collector for every 85-100 delinquent accounts. Salespeople or other dealership employees often don't have the time, desire or training to effectively collect payments.

An important tool in BHPH collections is the use of a GPS/Starter Interrupt device. The starter interrupt device is an extremely effective communication device. When the customer knows they need to make satisfactory arrangements with you or the car won't start, they will answer your calls and even call you, lowering both your delinquency and your collection expense. The GPS makes locating your vehicle for repossession much easier. Many small and midsize BHPH dealers will have their capital provider do most of the collection work, while still allowing the customers to pay at the lot. This has the advantage of having professionally trained collectors handling the telephone collections and activating starter interrupt device warnings and shutoffs. For dealers using Ace Motor Acceptance Corp as their capital provider, this can all be done while still having the customers make their payments at your dealership – the very essence of BHPH.

The Consumer Finance Protection Bureau now monitors BHPH dealers closely. It is very important when dealing with customers that a written Complaint Management System is created to identify, acknowledge, and resolve all customer complaints that occur. It is also very important that when a customer's car is repossessed, all appropriate forms and disclosures are sent to the customer based on laws in your state. An attorney who is familiar with collections and repossession laws can be a great source of information. Any third party repossession company should be vetted to see that they are properly licensed, bonded or insured.

Customer Care - Building your Customer Base

Successful BHPH dealers develop a strong base of repeat and referral business. Some of the key factors in building this base include the following: selling good quality vehicles, proper deal structures, helping customers with mechanical problems, collections practices that are firm but fair, treating customers with respect and asking for referrals.

Selling Quality Vehicles

Nothing kills repeat business as fast as bad merchandise. You need to sell vehicles that are in sound mechanical condition. Successful BHPH dealers have averaged $985 in reconditioning expense per car sold according to the NCM Benchmark. Successful BHPH dealers recondition both your purchased inventory and trade-in vehicles.

Proper Deal Structures

When a customer comes on your lot, start the sales process by gathering information. Determine what the customer's needs are in a vehicle (i.e. 5 kids at home will require a 6 or 7 passenger vehicle). Next find out how much down payment is available and determine what payment fits their budget. Select 3 units that meet these requirements and tell the customer, "Great news! I have 3 cars that are just what you're looking for. Let's look at all 3 and pick the one you want to take home." Choosing 3 cars generally works best because you are giving them choices (but not too many) so they do not feel like they are being pushed into something they don't want. Customers will frequently ask about more expensive vehicles. Never say, "You can't afford that," but do say "to keep the payment on that where you want it to be, would require a couple thousand dollars more down payment. Is that something you want to look at today?" It is important to say it sincerely and never sarcastically. Occasionally they can come up with substantially more down payment for their "Dream Car."

Helping Customers with Mechanical Problems

When your customers have mechanical problems, and they will, it is important to help them. If the car quits running, your customer will quit paying. This does not mean just opening your checkbook, but it does mean working with them. Several options are to discount the repairs, provide free labor with the customer providing the parts, or to defer a payment or two to the end of the contract. Providing free oil changes and taking care of minor issues throughout the contract are also good tools to both reduce repossessions and increase repeat business.

Collection Practices that are Firm but Fair

Collection practices must be firm but fair. Collectors should always determine the reason for delinquency and work with a customer who has a legitimate and believable reason. For instance, a customer's payment is due on Tuesday but they want to pay you on Friday. Accept their promise and do not activate the starter interrupt. Another example would be a customer who has already broken two promises and has not called you. In this case, you would activate the starter interrupt and require payment before allowing the car to start again. Firm but Fair!

Treating Customers with Respect

Many satisfied customers will refer friends and relatives to your dealership without you asking them. Treating customers with respect through every contact with the customer will lead to satisfied customers. Many opportunities exist to do this including when a customer is making a payment, when your collector contacts them, or when their car is in for service. Satisfied customers will lead to increased repeat business and referral sales. While many customers will give referrals on their own, it also helps to ask them if they know anyone looking for a car.

By working with the right capital provider and by implementing the Five Keys to Success discussed above, BHPH dealers at all experience levels will see changes for the better.

SPARE PARTS...NOTES

BIO: RUSS ALGOOD
CEO
Ace Motor Acceptance Corporation (AMAC)

Russ Algood is the CEO of Ace Motor Acceptance Corporation (AMAC) headquartered in Matthews, NC since 1998. He has been directly involved in the automobile business as either a dealer or in providing financing to automobile dealers for nearly 40 years!

Mr. Algood started as a BHPH dealer in Bloomington, Indiana in 1976 and in less than 10 years grew the operation to 5 BHPH locations and 5 franchise dealerships. In 1988 he was a co-founder of General Acceptance Corporation (GAC) a sub-prime auto finance company which went public in 1995. GAC expanded into 23 states and added 12 BHPH locations prior to being sold to Conseco in 1998. That is when Mr. Algood founded AMAC in Matthews, NC.

AMAC now operates throughout Southeast and Mid Atlantic states. Mr. Algood used his extensive experience as a dealership and finance company owner to develop and introduce the BHPH in a Box™ program.

Mr. Algood earned his Bachelor Degree in Business Administration and Management from Indiana University's Kelley School of Business. In addition he attended General Motor's Institute's Dealer Training program and was a member of an NADA 20 group. He was elected to the Board of the Indiana Automobile Dealers Association and helped to develop the association's ethics in advertising standards. As an independent auto dealer he was also a member of a Leedum 20 group, and of an auto finance company 20 group.

He has had articles published in the Used Car Dealer, the official magazine of the NIADA and numerous state Independent Auto Dealer Association magazines. Russ Algood brings a wealth of experience in both dealership and finance company operations, which is one reason why AMAC is an industry leader uniquely positioned to help the BHPH dealer grow their business.

Contact Information:
Russ Algood
AMAC
(T) 704-882-7100 (ext.7509)
Website: www.acemotoracceptance.com

ACE MOTOR
ACCEPTANCE CORPORATION

Recognizing the keys to the BHPH dealer's success, AMAC developed BHPH in a Box™. This program includes tools to support the keys to success for a BHPH dealer by providing:

- Funding for contracts
- Bulk Purchases
- Floor planning for inventory
- Underwriting and deal structure guidelines
- Training programs
- Collections – We collect or you collect
- Reports package provided
- Customers may pay at the lot
- Insurance tracking
- Discounted GPS / Starter Interrupt Systems
- Discounted Gap & Service Contracts

AMAC offers you a single-source solution that simplifies your operations while promoting your success.

The AMAC "BHPH in a Box™" program is available to dealers in North Carolina, South Carolina, Florida, Virginia, Alabama, Tennessee, Georgia, New Jersey, Maryland and Delaware. AMAC is forecasting expansion of this service into several neighboring states in the near future. **Anyone wanting more information can contact AMAC at 704-882-7100 (ext. 7509) or visit their website at www.acemotoracceptance.com.**

CHAPTER NINE

How to Present Your Portfolio to Receive the Most Floor Planning Dollars

By Bob Earle

The automotive industry is very unique in that it is one of the few industries where commercial loans are abundant and relatively easy for which to qualify. Whether you are just starting out or looking to grow your business, it is likely you will be able to find the capital needed to stock your dealership. Yet while there is a good chance you will be able to acquire a floor plan line of credit, the size of that line of credit will vary depending on business needs and overall portfolio snapshot.

Floor Plan 101: The Basics

First and foremost, to qualify for a floor plan, you need to have credit. Specifically, you should have a history of utilizing and repaying debt. Bad credit and hiccups on credit history aren't always deal-breakers, but they will likely reduce the amount for which you qualify. Additionally, there is a good chance that credit issues will have a negative impact on pricing structure. The good news is that over time, with good performance coupled with adherence to the terms and conditions, it is possible to eventually overcome these setbacks.

Over-extension is another red flag that should be avoided. Having credit cards that are maxed out, even if they aren't paid late, shows irresponsibility towards one's financials. Handling available credit responsibly is essential, so be sure to maintain a substantial amount of available credit.

Getting Started

So how does one go about opening up a dealership? First, any person considering opening a dealership should setup a free consultation with the floor plan company of their choosing right away. Even if you are well capitalized out of the gate, having a floor plan line of credit is a powerful asset that can help you seize opportunities as they arise. If you aren't well capitalized, you will probably be looking at starting with a smaller initial line of credit to get your business off the ground. As you turn inventory and build up your reserves, you can then submit a formal request for a credit line increase.

How to Use Your Floor Plan

It is relatively easy to use your floor plan line of credit. At most National Automotive Auction Association (NAAA) -affiliated auctions accept floor plan companies, the lender handles much of the back-door operations, so that leaves you to worry about one thing: purchasing inventory.

On auction day, after checking in at the auction, you will want to go to the appropriate department at the auction to check your credit availability with your floor plan lender(s). Once you are done bidding for the day, you will then take your blocked tickets to the auction check-out, where you will notify the auction which purchased units you wish to floor plan. From there, your floor plan company will take care of the rest.

Growing Your Business

If you are looking to grow your business through the addition of a floor plan line of credit, there are several items that will factor into the lending decision above and beyond your personal credit history. Trade references, business credit, equity, cash flow and the overall viability of your business all come into the picture and become increasingly important as you look to acquire more floor planning dollars.

Some dealers have substantial business equity and this is a great asset. To a floor plan company, inventory that is owned outright is viewed similarly to cash and is a good indicator of the viability of your operation. Business equity exhibits an enhanced capacity to repay debt. When applying for a floor plan, take the time to validate your equity position. Your floor plan company might ask to see the titles and bills of sale for all units that you currently own. They might even ask to physically inspect your owned inventory. This will all play into your favor as finance companies like to lend to people that already have money. The more equity you have, the lower the perceived risk.

Maintaining Your Business

For many dealers, once they get over the hump of actually starting their dealership, the biggest challenge that remains is being able to maintain their business. As with any business venture, there are certain concepts you need to keep in mind to make sure that you are keeping your business viable.

1) Know when to turn your vehicles

A term that is thrown around in the industry is velocity, which is the rate at which a dealer should turn their inventory. It is a simple concept: the longer a vehicle sits on your lot, the greater the risk that vehicle becomes. A point which the NIADA's Director of Dealer Development, Joe Lescota, stresses in NIADA's Certified Master Dealers course is that dealers should not keep a vehicle on the lot for more than 45 days.

2) Buy smart

It might be tempting to buy that snazzy sports car because it looks nice, but is it a good price and does it make a potential profitable addition to your inventory? Going to auction with a plan of how much you are willing to spend can help save you from those "impulse buys" that may turn into buyer's remorse down the road.

Another thing to keep in mind is that different cars sell better in different seasons. In the summer, you may get more business for convertibles, recreational vehicles and motorcycles than for trucks and SUVs. Make sure you're buying vehicles that will sell well to your customer base and won't be sitting on your lot.

3) Be more efficient with the use of working capital
Floor planning is a great way to balance credit and working capital to maximize your cash flow. This balancing act is often-times the lifeblood of a dealer's business and the fuel for growth. However, ineffective use of working capital and under-capitaliza-tion, among other factors, can contribute to a dealer going out of business because they can't keep up with their working capital. Simply put, the more cars you buy and sell, the greater the need to manage your cash flow.

4) Recognize the importance of your cash flow
It is a well-known fact that exhibiting cash flow is important, as it shows your ability to handle money. However, while many dealers can typically tell whether or not they made a profit for the month, they don't know how they got there. It is important to look at what your money is going towards in your business, because dealers that don't understand their cash flow end up fall-ing into the red. Taking the time to figure out how much you are spending on advertising, maintenance and other business costs can be the difference between a dealer that makes money versus a dealer that just gets by.

Larger Lines of Credit (Heavy Hitters)
When seeking a floor plan line of credit in excess of a half mil-lion dollars, both business and personal financials will typically need to be presented in addition to your standard business docu-ments. These financials typically include the following:
1) Personal Financial Statement (required for each owner/signer)
2) Personal Tax Return (2 years - required for each owner/signer)

3) Business Tax Return (2 years)
4) Business Bank Statements (3 months)
5) Income Statement (current and prior year-end)
6) Balance Sheet (current and prior year-end)

As you can imagine, the larger the credit line request, the more it will be scrutinized. Although you are welcome to provide a stack of photocopies, the best way to present your financials would be to scan them and then send the digital files via email or a USB thumb drive. Make sure everything is clearly labeled, and when applicable, provide more detail as opposed to less. Anything out of the ordinary should be accompanied by a letter of explanation.

In addition to the basic requirements, or if you are requesting a large line of credit (over $250k) to stock a start-up dealership, you should be prepared to provide some or all of the following:
1) Resume (for each owner/signer)
2) Photos of Dealership
3) Business Plan
4) Pro Forma Financial Statements

Presenting Bank Statements

If you have had any NSF's (non-sufficient funds), these will need to be explained in detail. Similarly, you will want to make sure your business checking account exhibits positive cash flow, meaning that you have more money coming in than you have going out. Take note of your average daily balance. Hopefully this figure is strong enough to support the line of credit you are requesting. In an ideal world, 20-30 percent of your floor plan line of credit would be in the form of working cash in your business checking account at all times. If you fall short of that mark, business equity via owned inventory can help bridge the gap.

Personal Financial Statement

When it comes to your personal financial statement, ideally you would have some liquid assets. Cash, 401K, IRA, CD's, bonds, etc. are all desirable elements to have in your portfolio given that they are accessible or readily available to borrow against. This is ideal because it demonstrates that you have reserves in place to "weather the storm" should you encounter a few bad months or an unforeseen industry shift.

A word of caution: some dealer principals place an inordinate value on the shares of their dealership within their personal financial statement. Although this may beef up your net worth, a floor plan lender will probably not take that into consideration. The "real" value of your business is predicated on what a buyer is willing to pay for it. Hence, the stated value on your personal financial statement is merely hypothetical on paper. And bear in mind that if your dealership were to go into a default status, your shares probably wouldn't be worth much at that point.

Another item to keep in mind is that if all of your assets are in the form of equities against mortgaged real estate, you may encounter difficulties with potential lenders. Banks have become skeptical of real estate equities given the recent real estate crisis. High dollar homes and commercial properties are slow to move and hard to appraise. Don't over estimate your real estate equity on your financial statements. Be realistic. Conversely, if your property is actually worth $500k and you only owe $100k on your mortgage, this would be an entirely different story. Having minimally leveraged or free and clear real assets should comfort a lender to some extent.

Income Statements

The income statement can be quite revealing, and often is used in part to determine what the true business need is when it comes to setting a floor plan credit limit. For instance, if a dealer were to a request a $500k line of credit but only turned $500k in gross sales last year, that request would surely be denied unless there were some major material changes in the operation that justified the increase. Additionally, this statement shines a spotlight on the overall sophistication of the operation. If you are generating additional revenues from F&I (finance & insurance) products and repairs for instance, that will all be itemized on this statement.

Balance Sheet

Simply put, the less you OWE and the more you OWN, the lower the credit risk. Again, lenders like to lend when the probability of repayment is the highest. Having too few assets and too much debt can become a downward spiral towards insolvency.

Pitfalls to Avoid

Floor plan companies are discretionary lenders, and it should be understood that your account is constantly being underwritten. Changes in your performance or credit profile will not go unnoticed. You can rest assured that commercial lenders have learned a lot about managing and mitigating risk, especially over the course of the last five years. It is crucial that you closely adhere to your lender's terms and conditions. NSF's, late curtailments, slow payoffs, and bad audits will inevitably prevent you from gaining the additional buying power you need to grow your business. Stay on top of managing your account, be honest and communicative, and you shouldn't have any problems.

It is also important to stay up-to-date on the industry. Recent changes in regulations have caused dealers to come under heat from the Consumer Financial Protection Bureau (CFPB) for compliance issues. What is most concerning is that the majority of dealers are not aware of these changes and the increased government focus on the industry. Dealers that are found to be non-compliant could face fines or possibly criminal charges.

Therefore, it is important that you take advantage of all the different resources from the NIADA and your state association to learn what the changes in regulation mean and what you need to do to stay compliant.

Never Been a Better Time Than Now...

The competitive landscape and modern technology have intersected, creating an environment that is more customer-friendly and efficient than ever before. In the past, many dealers chose to employ a person specifically charged with the task of managing the floor plan payoffs, audits, curtailment payments, and more. Today, most floor plan companies offer several tools designed to make the process of managing your account much simpler. In most cases, your account can be managed online or via a smartphone application. Robust reporting, performance metrics, payment management, and even the ability to view copies of titles and bills of sale are quickly becoming the norm, making floor planning more attractive than ever before. And when it comes to technology, as always, the best is yet to come...

In Conclusion

All of this ties into the overall viability of your operation. A thriving business should be building equity while reducing debt. A thriving dealer principal should be building net worth, not acquiring debt to keep his business above water. If your business isn't building and growing, then you probably shouldn't be seeking more floor plan dollars. More flooring won't turn around a failing business model. You would just be adding more fuel to the fire. Instead, focus on perfecting your operation. However, if your business is building equity and turning a profit, having some additional buying power can surely help you shift into the next gear.

SPARE PARTS...NOTES

BIO: BOB EARLE
South Atlantic Regional Director
NextGear Capital

Bob Earle serves as the South Atlantic Regional Director for NextGear Capital. He is responsible for the management and oversight of all aspects of NextGear Capital's business in the South Atlantic region, including the hiring and training of Account Executives. Bob has more than 25 years of leadership experience within the finance industry serving in numerous capacities with Avco Financial Services, Chase Bank and Citigroup where he was responsible for the largest Citigroup office in the state of Ohio.

In 2005, Bob joined Dealer Services Corporation as a General Manager and was quickly promoted to Regional Vice President of the North East region. Currently Bob manages the South Atlantic region, one of the largest regions in the company.

Bob has been instrumental in developing the NextGear Capital Leadership Program and the current Portfolio Management process.

In addition to serving as a presenter for Auction Academy, Bob is a two-time winner of Citigroup's prestigious Chairman's Forum Award, a recipient of the National Shared Responsibilities Award for Excellence in Growth, Compliance and Community Involvement and a certified Ambassador CMD.

NextGear Capital is the world's leading independent inventory finance company, providing flexible lines of credit for dealers to purchase new and used inventory throughout the U.S., Canada and the U.K.

NextGear Capital delivers innovative solutions that empower dealers to buy and sell inventory with versatile lines of credit that can be used at over 1,000 auto and specialty auctions and other inventory sources. The company offers floor plan financing for nearly any type of remarketed unit in automotive retail, wholesale, salvage and specialty, including recreational vehicles and trailers, marine, powersports, used heavy trucks, auto salvage and auto daily rentals.

The company also provides a robust array of services and support allowing dealers to acquire and sell more inventory. This includes state-of-the-art online and mobile account management tools, market-specific industry and dealer performance data, title services, records management and collateral protection.

The company is headquartered in Carmel, Indiana and is part of the Cox Automotive group of companies, which includes AutoTrader.com, Kelley Blue Book, Manheim and vAuto. Visit www.nextgearcapital.com to learn more. Website: www.acemotoracceptance.com

CHAPTER TEN
Implementing an Effective Payment Assurance Program

By Allen Douglas

We have a few horses and occasionally attend clinics around the country where we learn better ways to handle and manage horses. Clinton Anderson is a world-renowned horse trainer and I attended one of his clinics a few years ago. Clinton was presented with a horse he had never seen, brought in by his owner because this horse simply would not get on a horse trailer. I did wonder at that moment how the horse got there if he would not get on a trailer. The use of a stock trailer, which a more open trailer designed for cattle and other livestock, and lots of coaching, pulling, prompting, and tugging by the owner, made that happen. In any event, the horse trailer in the arena was so frightening to this horse that he actually shook when prompted to even go close to it.

Clinton looked at the audience, and asked, "How would you like to see, within one hour, me simply point to this trailer, and have the horse get on it?" We all thought he was crazy. There was no way this could happen! It was quite obvious the fear this horse had of that trailer.

Well, for one hour I watched Clinton work. He progressively and diligently, worked the horse in the arena. He went back and forth while all the time getting closer and closer to the trailer. He began to teach this horse that outside, in the arena, was a lot of work. Every time he got close to the trailer, Clinton let the horse rest; so the horse soon began to learn that the trailer meant rest. At the end of that hour, he pointed to the trailer, and the horse trotted just to the right spot. The crowd applauded!

Behavior Modification in this horse, taught by Clinton, created a completely different mindset and a totally opposite action to anything he had done before. This chapter will focus on how you should use this same technique, and realization, in all your operation.

What is GPS and payment assurance technology?

GPS (Global Positioning System) is technology that became fully functional in 1995 and originally operated on 24 satellites. The technology was initially developed and used primarily by the military. Today its use is about 50/50 between military and Department of Transportation (DOT). In the mid 1990's, development for consumer use gained prominence as private companies began exploring navigation software and mapping. Payment assurance technology was put into use in the early 1990s. This system consisted of devices installed in vehicles that required the input of a code you received as you made your payments on your installment loan. Without the code, your vehicle would not start, therefore, the motivation to keep payments current. As technology advanced, code fatigue took its toll on the older systems, and GPS systems developed the ability to provide payment motivation through reminder notices and starter interrupt technology (SID) while delivering location information and travel history, at the same time.

Who should use GPS and SID technology?

There are several factors that one must consider when analyzing the possible use of this technology; not the least of which is starting with a well thought out business plan that defines your key financial objectives and overall business model. Are you going to offer in-house financing? Will you use outside finance companies that require you to buy back (recourse) the loan in the event of a default? Any financial transaction that leaves you with some exposure on the loan is the most logical reason to utilize this technology. Obviously, a finance operation of any type will gain direct benefit and greatly improve collection operations and techniques.

The difference in how you decide to utilize this technology and its various features will start with your business plan and overall goals. It is widely accepted that, used properly, the full realm of features can greatly improve overall collection effectiveness, increase employee effectiveness by serving a greater number of customers, and improve cash flow.

Behavior Modification – The Key to Success

Possibly the greatest single thought to be sure you understand is behavior modification. Most individuals reading this and contemplating in-house financing, will naturally think of this as behavior modification in their customer who owes the outstanding note on the vehicle. While this is true and is extremely important for you to understand how to properly motivate your customer, just as important in today's environment, is behavior modification of your own employees and entire staff. We will explore both these concepts in this section.

Motivating your customer to perform on their note should be the major focus of your entire organization. From your lot person to the owner, EVERYONE must be completely ready to satisfy that customer on an individual and daily basis. It starts from the first conversation with that customer, and continues long after the sale until the note is completely satisfied; whether paid off or traded on another vehicle. After all, if you carry your own paper (finance your own sales) you are NOT in the car business. You are truly in the cash and finance business. Customer service and satisfaction are the ONLY ways you will gain the greatest opportunity to make every customer a success story. It is quite easy to sell a vehicle, but the most successful operation, will embrace the fact that unless they maximize their collections, they will have a very difficult time sustaining, must less growing, their business. Customer behavior modification starts right at the closing of the sale, and the most opportune time to gain the most impact is during the disclosure portion concerning your GPS and SID system. We will completely cover proper disclosure later, but for now, you MUST realize that what you do and say at this time speaks volumes to your customer. We were all children once and tested our parents. But I was a boy that really tested the limits of what was expected of me. I found out, as I suspect you did, that when the line was drawn in the sand, and the hammer came down, we were at the end of our boundaries and something unpleasant was about to come our way. This holds so true for your customer today. Like us as children, they must learn the 'boundaries' of what they can do. It is the complete task of your entire organization to train and educate your customer toward their expected behavior. While we will also cover best collection practices later, just know for now that if you give them 10 days, they will want 11. If you grant payment deferrals, they will always be expected. Be consistent from day one with the implementation and enforcement of your set, well defined, written company policies.

Gaining behavior modification in your staff is twofold. We have already mentioned the importance of customer contact from day one in a positive, serving manner. An attitude of customer satisfaction is quite necessary toward gaining the most effective payment performance, and today's legislative and enforcement climate in all of consumer finance is like no other time we have seen in our society. Consumer finance, and especially the automotive business, is viewed by some in our government as heavy handed toward the consumer. Some even call it 'usury' and an all out effort is being made to uncover deceptive, unfair, and abusive practices. Any operation today MUST maintain an attitude of compliance and customer satisfaction. You will hear many times the importance of well defined, written policies and procedures that are consistently enforced. The behavior of your staff will demonstrate the attitude of your business, directly impact your customer's performance and the perception given to regulating authorities. There is no substitute for setting up operations the proper way.

Installation – "Hide" & Security

The most advanced and strongest system with the best features will do you no good if installation time and procedure is shorted. Don't make the mistake of having the attitude of getting the installation process finished as quickly as humanly possible. While time and money are important, it is all too easy to rush the installer and prevent him from getting the system wired and placed properly. Remember, you want this system to serve you over the several years your loan will be outstanding with that particular customer. The difference in 20 minutes can mean a difference in years of quality service and performance with the right system. While the system must be wired properly, the most important factor, by far, is to properly 'hide' the system away. It will take longer, but yield a very significant difference in performance longevity. In addition, tamper rates (where a customer may remove or interfere with the system) are affected by two factors: Installation and Disclosure. Disclosure requires its own section and is talked about in detail.

A proper installation is one that provides:
(1) complete written instructions;
(2) personal training;
(3) step-by-step processes to insure the correct working order of the system; and
(4) proper testing of features like payment reminders and starter interrupt prior to the vehicle being placed for sale or delivered to a customer.

The electronics in today's vehicles are getting more and more advanced. Be sure your provider of these systems can properly train and help you trouble shoot any questions your installer may have concerning ignition wires, push button starters, and starter interrupt. In addition, proper training and set-up of security access by the installers must be in place. Installers must have access to only the vehicles they are working on, and should have no access to vehicles in the hands of customers.

Security of System Access – Permissions Granted

Now that the systems are installed and your staff knows what to do with them, you must decide who has access to what, and what functions they can perform. Part of your written procedures will include the responsibility of each employee with regard to this technology. Who can track vehicles'? Who can send payment reminders? Who can disable a vehicle's starter that prevents a vehicle from cranking? Each user of the system should be set up with his/her own username. This builds accountability and an audit trail of all commands issued to a vehicle. A proper system also is one that includes the ability for you to grant access and permissions by each individual user.

Remember that this system is a tool for use in protecting your assets and enforcing timely payments. It is NOT to be used for favors or casual tracking. A sales person who gets enamored with a customer that walks in and tracks them in order to find the places they visit in hopes of meeting them there is called "Stalking". A phone call received by an excited customer saying their car has been stolen and asking you to track the vehicle can be a domestic squabble in which you do not want to get involved. Tell the customer to call the police, file a report, and have the police contact you. Any situation like these outside the intended use of this system can leave your business exposed to severe liability. Proper use of the system will protect access to and the privacy of your customer.

One of the best ways to document that you are properly training your staff is the use of an Employee Training Document. This training procedure and resulting document should be used for ALL the policies and procedures of your business. It will outline the employees responsibilities, disclose the proper use of this technology, disseminate the company policies and procedures, inform them of what to do and what not to do, and be kept as written proof of proper training. It should be kept in the employees' personnel files. Be sure your provider of GPS/SID systems can properly advise you concerning this document.

Disclosure – A Must

Just a few years ago, there were few operators in this industry that wanted to disclose this technology. They wrongly interpreted disclosure as an invitation for a customer to tamper with the system, or a way to maintain an upper hand, when it came to collections and recovery of the vehicle. These and any other so called justifications not to disclose this technology is only a recipe for disaster. It is true that, as of this writing, there is no federal mandate that requires disclosure, and only five states maintain a requirement or attitude that you must disclose. These facts are also very misleading if it leads you to any consideration not to disclose. The Consumer Finance Protection Bureau (CFPB), the Federal Trade Commission (FTC), Department of Justice (DOJ), and local Attorney General will hold a greatly different opinion on this topic. Today the search by these regulators toward finding those operators that are deceptive, unfair, or abusive is active, serious, and very close to where you operate.

Regardless of the motivations of these agencies, I know that the best way for you to maximize your operations and collections begins with the disclosure process-IT IS THE START OF EFFECTIVE COLLECTIONS. This is the first opportunity to begin the behavior modification and training we discussed. This should be a positive experience and add to that enjoyed excitement of the vehicle purchase. The disclosure process, properly deployed, will solve 50% - 60% of your collection problems BEFORE they occur. Your staff involved in the disclosure process must be properly trained in what to say and what not to say. Again, remember the employee training process and document. Your provider should be able to provide you a suggested discloser document that should be reviewed by your attorney to insure it is proper for use in your particular jurisdiction. It should be signed and witnessed as part of your closing sales documentation.

Underwriting

The underwriting process of approving a loan is not to be taken lightly. As good as our technology is, it will NEVER replace a good underwriting policy. You can finance everyone, but you will also repossess a lot of vehicles. A good business plan is one that defines a process and business operation that promotes longevity in revenue, profit, customer satisfaction and retention, and community involvement.

A good underwriting policy will define, in writing, the requirements needed by a consumer to purchase a vehicle. Factors can include geography (how far from the dealership do they live), down payment amount, down payment percentage, credit history, work history, etc. You may have multi-level programs that provide different levels of benefits for customers that qualify. For example, customers with better credit history may qualify for a lower interest rate. Larger down payments may qualify them for better terms. Any number of quantifiable characteristics may allow the use of these multi-level programs. It is extremely important that all policies and loan requirements are applied consistently among all sales transactions. If you do offer different programs, they must be solidly founded on easily quantifiable terms, and applied consistently to all customers, so as to not discriminate in any way between loans.

The use and installation of GPS and SID systems should also be applied consistently within your portfolio. If you decide to use systems only on certain loans, it should be based on written, well-defined policies. Be prepared to justify the decision to only include systems on a portion of your loans and apply this policy consistently.

Written Policy on Delinquencies –
Best Collection Practices

I recommend to the owner of each company we consult with, to decide early on as to what their appetite is for delinquencies within their portfolio. It is a given fact that within any finance operation delinquencies WILL exist. This is a portion (a very important one) of your business that you must completely understand, recognize, and manage to precise levels. As it has already been stated, if you are financing, you are not in the car business, but the cash and finance business. The importance you place on collections will directly impact the success of your overall business. The technology offered by GPS and SID systems have a tremendous impact on reducing delinquencies as long as they are used properly, and applied consistently.

Always start with a written policy concerning your collections procedure, and set your target for maximum allowed delinquencies. While it may seem contrary to you, to say you will allow certain levels of past due amounts, it very important to recognize that this is a natural part of finance operations. Managing this number to your specifically designed acceptable levels will keep you focused on overall success and not emotionally entangled with surprise levels of past due accounts.

Everyone would prefer that they have no account that would ever go even one day past due. Since this is not the real world, you must manage this to your desired and acceptable level. To develop your tailored goal, examine the factors that surround you. What are the requirements of your state? How long of a grace period is mandated by your state or included in your installment contract? This will give you a starting point. A grace period is the amount of time after the contractual due date that you are required to allow the customer to make their payment. This can vary widely by state. Periods of no requirement to 30 days can be mandated and allow you no option to act sooner. For example, in South Carolina, when an account goes past due, you may send a notice to the customer only after they are 10 days past due. On the 11th day, you send the past due notice advising the customer to remit their payment, and then you must allow them another 20 days to 'cure' this default in their installment contract. This is known as a "Right to Cure" clause. Again, this grace or cure period does vary from state to state, so be sure you consult with your State association and attorney to learn the requirements for the area in which you are operating.

Another common mistake made in managing a portfolio is the policy and actions regarding partial payments. It is very easy, when allowing the consumer to appeal to your human side, to grant extensions (payment deferrals), or take a partial payment toward the loan. They can be very convincing that they just can't make all the payment right now. At this juncture, the first thing you should remember is our discussion on 'Behavior Modification'. This is a crucial point where you will train the customer on what is allowed. It is common that eighty-five percent (85%) of the people that ask for a partial payment or payment deferral do not need it. This is simply the way they manage their money. A payment deferral, of any type, granted from anyone money is owed to, means they now have more dollars to spend elsewhere. There are two things you should ask when this request comes from a customer. First ask, "Why is this needed?" You have a right to know what is causing them to default on their contract, and secondly, "when will it be caught up?"

Another common mistake, after the first one of allowing a partial payment, is to not have a definitive time to catch up the payment. Train your customer that this is not acceptable behavior and must be remedied. Not asking these two questions will easily put you into a scenario where one deferral request turns into two, and so on. This situation will perpetuate throughout the entire loan like a cancer and the loan will never come back to a current state. I have seen situations where so many deferral requests have been granted that the customer is now so far upside down that it is impossible for them to remedy it. Be very cautious with partial payments. Have a defined policy and stick with it.

Use of Payment Reminder Warnings and Starter Interrupt

A very important part of your collection procedures revolves around how you use payment reminders and starter interrupt technology to motivate payments. A payment reminder is the ability to send to the vehicle an audible sound (beep or buzzing) that is heard each time the vehicle is started. A starter interrupt is just that. It allows you to disable the customers' ability to start the vehicle. Remember our discussion on Disclosure and how it is the start of effective collections? During that time you explained, in a positive way, that the 'computer' will notify the customer in the event you need to talk with them perhaps about their payment, insurance, etc. When they hear this sound (which can be played from your office computer) they should give you a call as soon as possible. If it is a Friday afternoon at 3:00 pm and they don't call before closing, the 'computer' may do something crazy like disable the vehicle. Create a sense of urgency in that customer to give you a call quickly. Remember the horse being trained to want to be in the trailer? The customer needs to understand that the safe place for them is talking with you. This is the essence of the behavior modification we have talked about.

In the event a payment reminder does not get their attention, the starter interrupt most certainly will. Just like not paying your electric bill and having the electricity shut off, the customer will quickly learn to prioritize their payments. They should first take care of their home. No, the vehicle is not first. If they don't have a home, they will most likely live in the car. No one wants a car after someone has lived in it. After taking care of and providing for a place to live, they should then take care of their transportation. There are many philosophies on the use of starter interrupt. Should the vehicle be disabled while they are at work, at home, in the middle of the night, riding down the road, or at a gas station? We disable the starter's ability to start the car, not the ignition. During the installation, this is tested to insure the actual operation of the vehicle is not affected in any way. Only after the vehicle is stopped and the ignition turned off, will the interrupt take effect. You must decide what your policy will be on when to use this feature. It can be one, or all, of the above. The purpose of this feature is to get the attention of the delinquent customer, not to debilitate them to the point of anger. Proper disclosure, reminder notices, phone calls, and letters, are all training tools. Behavior modification should have already taught them that this is a result of their actions and it can be quickly remedied by just calling you.

You must also know that the use of starter interrupt is being interpreted by most courts as a 'soft' repossession. Use of this technology must follow the cure laws (as explained under delinquencies) of the particular state you are in.

Define/Enforce Policies

As you manage your collection efforts based upon your written policies and procedures, remember this is a business. Keep the emotion out of your decisions. Create good policies for your operation, enforce them consistently, and do it in a nice, fair, but firm way. Drawing that line for behavior modification in a repeated consistent way, will let your customer know what is expected, prevent the huge emotional surprise, and the result will be a shorter path to the lowest delinquency possible. Consistency in all your operations, treating all customers equally, along with an active customer satisfaction procedure, will provide the greatest resource and preparation for any visit or inquiry from the CFPB, FTC, DOJ, or Attorney General. Be sure your Compliance Officer and Customer Relations Manager (they can be the same person) are well trained and actively involved in all your operations. They should take the lead in setting that positive attitude and atmosphere of compliance throughout your entire organization.

Also, during any collection period, while contacting your customer for payment, you must follow guidelines set by the Fair Debt Collection Practices Act (FDCPA). These are guidelines concerning the time and frequency that you may contact a customer concerning a delinquent account and the proper manner in which you conduct your collection efforts. Become familiar with these guidelines and include them in your employee training.

Written Repossession Policy

As good as your collection efforts will be, another fact of any finance operation, is that not everyone will make their payments in an acceptable way. Therefore, you will have to repossess some vehicles, and you need policies on how that will happen. Some factors to consider are:
(1) Are you actively communicating with your customer?
(2) Are they making some payments?
(3) How long are they delinquent?
(4) How much in dollars are they delinquent?
(5) Has insurance lapsed?

All these, and others you may discover in your operation, are quantifiable ways you can define a written policy on vehicle repossession. Remember to apply your policies consistently across all your customers. Keep the emotion out. Do not create any situation that might be interpreted as a discriminatory act against a customer that just pressed your buttons and caused a knee-jerk reaction. Be nice, fair, but firm and consistent.

Written Redemption Policy

In the event a customer would like to redeem, or make good their note after you have repossessed their vehicle, decide your actions based on your written redemption policy. What does the customer need to do? You can set the rules for how this might happen. Should you require them to:

(1) pay off the note,

(2) only catch up delinquent payments,

(3) pay for the recovery fees and delinquent payments, or

(4) If they did not have a GPS or SID system installed, you can do it at this point. They have already proven to be a bad payer and you could use the additional technology to turn them around. Go through the Disclosure procedure, and get the Disclosure document signed. Start the Behavior Modification training and re-educate your customer. I have seen the worst payers turn into the best payers by using this opportunity correctly.

Any, and all of these options are available to you. Again, apply your actions consistently with everyone.

Technology and Collections

As you now know, technology that exists today is far more advanced than any other time in our industry. We, at STARS GPS specialize in understanding the collection and compliance aspect of your operation. We provide, not just the strongest hardware possible working over the largest network, but also the resources to better assist you in raising your operational awareness to a higher level of understanding on how to maximize the use of our technology, and maintain compliance. I encourage you to consider contacting a company like STARS GPS that provides this type of technology and training. It will help you create a more efficient and effective operation.

SPARE PARTS...NOTES

BIO: R. ALLEN DOUGLAS
Founder/President
STARS GPS

An industry veteran since 2005, Mr. Douglas is Founder and President of STARS GPS. His educational background includes degrees in Business, Accounting, and Economics. These coupled with high level Sales, Marketing, and Behavioral Training, gives Mr. Douglas a complete foundational basis to understand, interpret, and apply key issues facing finance operations and dealerships in today's automotive industry. As the National Independent Automobile Dealers Association's (NIADA) Exclusive National Corporate Partner for GPS and Starter Interrupt technology, STARS GPS is also working diligently to assist operators with an understanding of today's legislative climate within our industry.

Douglas and STARS GPS maintain a focus on state-of-the-art technology, and training that is just as intense. Overall emphasis on asset protection, compliance, disclosure, employee training, effective collection practices, customer motivation and payment behavior modification, are all relevant topics that are all enhanced with our technology. Offering the strongest hardware, broadest communication coverage available, and enhanced collection features enables the smallest of finance operations to become the most efficient and current with the least amount of effort.

In addition to our national partnerships, STARS GPS also has Exclusive relationships with over 12 state IADA's whereby we provide GPS and Starter Interrupt technology. We understand the importance of IADAs and their primary role to aid the local dealer. The effects of the efforts of a local body of fellow operators coming together to face current issues, influence local legislators, build a common alliance, & create educational opportunities learning from each other, cannot be underestimated.

We are in a significant growth trend and are blessed to have the opportunity to serve our industry. We are very grateful for the faith, recognition, and relationship bestowed on us by NIADA and many state associations. Our drive is to daily serve this industry with the utmost respect, professionalism, and state-of-the-art systems.

Contact Information:
R. Allen Douglas
STARS GPS, LLC
(T) 877-828-4770

CHAPTER ELEVEN
Pay Me Now or Pay Me Later
By John Brown

When it comes to joining organizations, many business owners pass up on a higher return on investment (ROI) because of lack of knowledge or because they refuse to join their industry trade group. It doesn't stop at associations that represent your business professionally. It includes other related organizations such as the local Chamber of Commerce, the Rotary Club, and other similar organizations. Both professional and social organizations play an increasing part in making us better business people and more profitable auto dealers. As the age old adage says, we are here to help you.

In any industry, the best of the best belong to associations and groups that will help make them better. Warren Buffet, one of the world's best investors, belongs. Donald Trump is a member. Oprah Winfrey does. Mark Zuckerberg is socially connected and even one of the most valuable brands in the world belongs. Rolls-Royce and its founders, Charles Rolls and Sir Henry Royce, knew the value of belonging to organizations that can help you grow your business.

Many business owners say they do not have time, nor do they get any value from being a member of various organizations. Hog wash. When given a chance and provided with the right information, these owners are quickly converted to believers. Many business owners fail, for all sorts of reasons, but most often because you do not know what you do not know. That's just one way that associations can help.

If you do not have enough customers, maybe joining an organization where you can meet prospective buyers would provide a positive ROI. If you fall out of compliance with various regulations that you did not even know about, would the investment of membership fees provide an ROI? If you think the cost of compliance is expensive, try paying hefty fines for non-compliance. If you need access to more suppliers or less expensive suppliers, more capital to grow your business, information about the latest marketing trends or even access to knowledgeable accountants and lawyers, wouldn't the ROI be better than no ROI?

Tracy Myers, owner of Frank Myers Auto, a former President of the Carolinas Independent Automobile Dealers Association, and one of the leading used car dealers in the USA, wants you to know that "The greatest benefit of being a member in an association is the networking and camaraderie that goes on among members. Associations let you know what's going on in your industry and as a member, you, your employees and your business will benefit. If you have the resources, the more associations and working groups you can join, the more you will benefit. But at a minimum everyone should be a member of the organization that represents their given industry. For independent automobile dealers that organization is the CIADA or your state's Independent Automobile Dealers Association (IADA) and the National Independent Automobile Dealers Association (NIADA)."

Membership in trade associations not only benefits you and the employees of your company, but it also projects a positive image of your firm to your customers. Membership in associations shows a business' initiative. Your business engagement with a particular trade group indicates your seriousness to learn all you can about your industry. Involvement with local community groups allows you to meet potential customers and shows you're going to be around for a long time. Business changes so rapidly in today's environment, to be able to meet the ever changing demands of the market you serve, you must have access to up-to-date information. The association is the least expensive way to show your commitment and stay current with change. Customers, when given knowledge about your membership in various organizations, are much more likely to buy from you, often two out of three times more likely, according to some surveys.

Darryl Jackson, Owner of Crown Auto Sales and Finance, is an active participant in the automotive industry and in the CIADA. Jackson indicates that he gains valuable insight into changes with regulations by being a member. "As an owner, I'm held responsible for everything that takes place at my three locations. Having the Association as a partner to update me on various changes that take place almost on a daily basis with the Consumer Financial Protection Bureau (CFPB), the Federal Trade Commission (FTC), and so on, is only one reason I'm involved. The government would like to completely regulate the Buy Here Pay Here (BHPH) dealer out of business and so that's why I take an active part in legislative issues with the Association. Additionally, I am able to use the annual meeting weekend to incentivize my management team to learn and produce more by having my employees and their partners attend the three-day conference, usually at a beach resort."

Conversely, surveys indicate that on average more businesses fail that are not members of their trade association. Coincidence? Maybe. Again, one of the biggest advantages of association membership is the networking and camaraderie that takes place among members. However, to benefit from this you must participate and be an active member within your association.

It's no secret that these are challenging economic times filled with uncertainty and increasing government regulations. This can either be a burden or it can be viewed as an opportunity. If you are a member of an organization that represents your interests, membership should seriously be part of your business success plan.

Warren Buffett said "Price is what you pay, value is what you get." It's all about the value of your investment. The business organizations you belong to should have as their number one priority, helping you grow your business.

As a fraternity brother of David Letterman (Sigma Chi) and a fan of his "Top Ten Lists," here are my top ten reasons why you should be a member of a professional association:

1. **What do you have to lose?** Plenty.

2. **Low cost of entry.** Membership within many of the leading organizations representing your industry is often the most cost effective tax-deductible expense you will have.

3. **Get the inside information.** When changes occur within the industry from a marketing, regulatory, pricing or consumer perspective, how do you find out about the changes? Better information means better decisions that can lead to better profitability.

4. **Know the regulators who govern your business.** Your business is faced with a mirage of regulation from every unit of government and practically every department- from local zoning regulations and licensing requirements, to state Department of Motor Vehicles (DMV) regulations, to the federal governments' increasing involvement in every aspect of your business.

5. **Advocacy.** Trade associations represent your professional interests. By advocating for many with the same interests, it is more cost effective and delivers better results than from going it alone.

6. **Public Relations.** As a group, car dealers have an image with the general public that is challenging. You can help change that image by being part of a larger group working daily to change that image.

7. **Grow Your Business.** Who better to help grow your business than to get best practices from dealers who are already successful?

8. **Never Stop Learning.** The best of the best never stop learning. Your trade association provides you with access to the best education to keep you in compliance and to help make you a better dealer.

9. **Access to the Best Vendors.** Don't go it alone. You need access to vendors to help you grow your business and become more profitable. With thousands of vendors serving an industry, you can't possibly find time to add to your already full schedule to vet your suppliers. Your trade association can do this for you. They already have relationships with vendors you can trust to help make you better and serve your dealership.

10. **Save Money.** When you join an association, your ROI is often higher than the products you sell. Enjoy discounts that can help you earn more money.

Let's examine each of these in a little more depth.

Plenty to lose. It's simple, but one of the hardest to recognize in your business plan. Sure, you can lose it all, go out of business, call it quits or just give up; however, it usually doesn't happen that way, that abruptly, or that quickly.

No it's more like a slow agonizing process. It might take months or years. It may not even look like the end when it begins. It might look like something simple to fix. Maybe you didn't sell as many cars this month as you wanted. Then this is followed by a decision to take a small loss on the car by selling it at the auction and moving it out of your inventory. This decision is followed by you buying a better car at the auction for a higher price than you know will sell on your corner lot. "Just put that on my floor plan please," you tell the auction.

"This one is a great car. Can't wait to get it cleaned up and on the lot. It will sell fast and for a better margin, to help cover my losses from the last deal," you tell yourself. Sure enough, it sells the second week on the lot, at a decent price and a good margin. Things are rocking now. This process mirrors itself time and time again.

Then you get that visit from the DMV inspector. After the inspection you say, "Fine? What fine? What violations? I've been doing this for years the same way and never had a problem."

Your trade organization hears it all the time.

If you were a member, maybe you would have known that the first car you bought, the one you couldn't sell, wasn't on the top selling list of reliable cars. In fact, it was on a recall list you never checked. But I bet your customers did. They checked online before even stepping foot on your lot. That's why it didn't sell. Your customer knew more than you did.

When you sold it at the auction for a loss, you didn't really remember to add up the real costs of the transaction in the first place: the buy/sell fees, the floor planning costs to carry the car, the time, effort and materials you spent keeping it in "showroom condition" on your lot, to name a few.

And that car you replaced it with that sold in less than two weeks? Yep, that one. You sold it without having the title in hand. "It should be here any day," you keep telling yourself. Now the DMV has found out. Selling a car without a title is against the law, even if you do it all the time. Oh, and that fine is for selling a car without a title.

The problems just keep on mounting and slowly but surely you reach that day that you just can't continue and you become a statistic by closing down. "It couldn't be avoided. I did what I had to do," you tell yourself.

You had plenty to lose. Not just the single transaction or the dealership itself. You lost your dream. You had plenty to lose. Why not be part of something that wants you to succeed and will help provide you with the tools you need to be successful. Need a list of the best selling cars, or a list of the ones to avoid? Ask your trade association. Need education about what is working from a marketing perspective to get that car sold? Ask your trade association for some ideas. Been doing something all along and didn't know you were doing it wrong? Have you ever attended a trade association sponsored education class?

So you have plenty to lose. Not just your dream, but there are lots of people counting on your success, particularly your family. Your trade association can help.

Low Cost of Entry. Joining your trade association should be one of the most cost effective things you do for your career. The return that the Association provides you should be simple and straightforward. It shouldn't take your accountant to tell you how one of the best investments you made also provides you with a great ROI. For example, the CIADA membership is just $285 per year.

That is less than one dollar a day, closer to 75 cents a day. CIADA is your least expensive employee. CIADA is one of your most knowledgeable employees. We work overtime on your behalf at no extra charge. We won't call in sick. We are there when you need us. Just a phone call away and we will even give you an 800 number to call us.

There are plenty of other organizations you can join. A few might cost you less, but most will charge you more. The CIADA is the most effective organization that represents you, the independent dealer. There is no other non-profit organization that is part of a leading national association that has as its sole purpose to represent the independent used car dealer. There is no extra charge to the dealer to be part of NIADA. The CIADA pays your membership fee to the NIADA!

Inside information. When changes occur within the industry, did you ever think of it as inside information? Or does it just seem that way. The DMV, the IRS, the CFPB, the FTC and all the rest of the countless number of other lawmakers and regulators who govern your business aren't going to send you information about the changes they just made. It gets treated like insider trading. But you're still responsible.

So when things do change, how will you find out about it? If you are a member of your trade association, that is one way you will find out about it. When the FTC changes the Buyers Guide or when the CFPB publishes a regulation that will affect your business, the CIADA will send out an email informing dealers of the changes. When the State Legislature initiates new laws that the DMV implements, the CIADA will notify dealers via email and postings on the CIADA website.

Things are constantly changing and the information doesn't have to be treated like insider knowledge.

Know the regulators who govern your business. Your business is faced with a mirage of regulation from every unit of government at all levels and from practically every department. Your trade association should have established relationships with many of these regulators and enforcement officials. By working closely with them, the member benefits in several ways.

One way is for your association to know about change when change occurs. Another advantage is for your association to be asked for input prior to a decision being made. Many ideas never see the light of day because your trade association knows the regulators and is able to stop a bad idea before it ever gets implemented.

Your association should have a presence with the main legislative body in your state. The CIADA proactively meets with legislators and has membership days at the State Capitol. By visiting with lawmakers while they are in session and when they are back home in their communities, relationships form and information and ideas are discussed before they ever get implemented into law.

The CIADA also partners with DMV officials to inform you of the proper procedures and latest changes with free Title and Registration sessions. This allows either the member or their professional staff to learn directly from the DMV as to what forms are needed, how to fill them out correctly and how to spend the least amount of time at their local DMV office. This alone is worth the price of membership in CIADA.

The CIADA doesn't stop working for you at the borders of the Carolinas. As part of the NIADA, CIADA members have the opportunity to go to Washington, DC, and meet with members of Congress and the Administration. To be able to speak directly to those who either pass the laws or implement the laws, is of tremendous value. If you ever said to yourself, "What were they thinking and if I could just have one minute to tell them (regulators and law makers) what we are really facing," then join your association because that is what we will help you do.

Advocacy. Who is going to represent your interests? You already said you were too busy. Already too regulated. It's tough enough to stay in compliance now, let alone what else might come down the pike. So if you aren't going to be your personal advocate, who will do it for you? That's why you should be a member of your trade association.

Trade associations represent your professional interests. By advocating for many with the same interests, it is more cost effective and delivers better results than from going it alone. If you would hire a lobbyist, the cost to you would be about the same as it is for the association. But the association has many members to spread the cost among, so it's more economical for your association to represent your views.

When you have multiple constituencies such as local, state and federal governments including elected officials at all three levels, it's nearly impossible for you to have an effective relationship with all of them. That is one of the reasons why your investment in your association has such a high ROI. Your association has the professional relationship and maintains those relationships to advocate on your behalf regardless of which political part is in power.

Public Relations. Used car dealers have a reputation that only members of Congress can say is worse than their own. But it doesn't have to be that way. Car dealers are among the least admired when asked to rate the honesty and ethical standards of people in different fields. You can help change that image by being part of a larger group working daily to change that image. Part of that image is undeserving. There are many, many dealers that are recognized in their home communities for all they do to enhance the lives of others. They are active members in their churches, their local school districts, the little league team, Girls Scouts and countless other organizations. They are recognized by their local Chambers of Commerce for years of providing a service that nearly everyone needs.

Being part of an association will provide you with access to positive public relations stories about dealers who care about their profession and are out there every day to make a difference and to do it right. They make sure the customer is satisfied not just for themselves, but for the reputation of the industry. By being part of the association, you can receive accolades to help position your business to customers who want to do business with the best.

Grow Your Business. Who wants to sell more cars, to make more money and be more than you ever thought you could be? MANY OF US! So who better to help grow your business than to get best practices from dealers who are already successful? Don't reinvent, learn it straight from the Masters.

When you are involved with your association you will have access to the very best in every aspect of your business. The very best sell more cars. The very best do the right things to stay in compliance and to make sure their customers are completely satisfied. The very best want to share their success with you. By helping you get better, they get better. When they get better and you get better, everyone benefits and you both grow your businesses.

Never Stop Learning. The best of the best never stop learning. Your trade association provides you with access to the best education to keep you in compliance and to help make you a better dealer. With changes occurring all the time, it's important to keep learning.

When you are a member of the CIADA, your continuing education (CE) requirements are free. That's right, members do not have to pay for state mandated continuing education classes as long as the annual membership is renewed during your annual CE training. You get more value for your membership dollar.

By being a member, you will also be able to attend education that is part of the NIADA curriculum. If you want to be among the best, you might consider becoming a Certified Master Dealer (CMD). CMDs are among the top one percent within the NIADA membership who have obtained the very best education that independent dealers can obtain.

NIADA also provides some of the very best education that an independent car dealer can find through various relationships with experts in the industry. There are countless opportunities for you to learn more about your profession, often at a discounted price for members. Additionally, the NIADA Annual meeting has the very best educational opportunities for members each year. There really isn't an excuse for not learning from the best in your industry.

Access to the Best Vendors. Your trade association can put you in contact with vendors who serve your industry. Whatever you need, your association can help you find it.

CIADA also offers you forms to keep you in compliance and complete your deal. Or we can connect you with some of the very best Dealership Management Systems (DMS) to make sure you don't have to hand print the VIN code on forms. Just use your smart phone and scan it into your computer, then to your buyers Bill of Sale and other required documentation.

Are you in the BHPH business? Then you should be using technology to protect your assets. We can connect you with the best in the Global Positioning System (GPS) business. Want to increase your prospects of getting your customer to pay on time? GPS can help you and CIADA can introduce you to the most knowledgeable BHPH dealers and experts in the industry.

Save Money. There are several ways you can earn your membership fee back and even more. If you are a CIADA member, you can get a quote from our Dealers Risk and Insurance Services (DRIS) for your required bond and garage liability insurance.

More often than not, DRIS is the low cost provider. DRIS can save you money and often we can save you enough to pay for your membership. It doesn't cost you anything to have CIADA/DRIS quote you a price, so what are you waiting for?

By being a member of CIADA you also get valuable coupons good at more than 40 auctions up and down the East Coast. Let's say you go to either the Manheim or Adesa auctions in the Carolinas. By attending either of these auctions and buying or selling just one vehicle each quarter, you will save enough money on these transactions to pay for your membership and then some.

Perhaps you don't go to the big auctions like Adesa or Manheim. Maybe you only go to the oldest auction in America - Rawls, or to Carolina Auto Auction in Anderson, SC, or maybe Charleston Auto Auction or Greensboro Auto Auction and Speedway North Carolina. Then that's great too, because at any of these auctions you save money. Only go to out-of-state auctions? Most likely we have you covered there, as well. So what's holding you back? Aren't you in the business to make money?

Being a member of your trade association is simple and easy. One phone call or search on the Internet will be all that is required to find a membership form and join. Your success is directly tied to the success of the trade association.

To realize the benefits and influence the direction of your association and your profession, you may need to get involved and contribute to the success of your dealership and your association. You will be encouraged to attend events such as Legislative Day in your state, annual meetings and recruit your colleagues to join the association. If you are interested in getting involved and becoming a board member, reach out and indicate your willingness to get involved. You can't expect to change the system unless you are in the system.

Your professional association gives you leverage and resources to meet your business needs. Information, advocacy, public relations, expanding opportunities and professional development, sales materials and gaining education to beat the competition. The only thing holding you back, the only thing between you and your continued success, is you.

SPARE PARTS...NOTES

BIO: JOHN BROWN
Executive Director, CIADA

John Brown currently serves as the Executive Director of CIADA. In this capacity, John is responsible for all aspects of the member-driven association. As a results-driven executive with experience at global automotive organizations, John also has a long and accomplished history in philanthropy and government relations as a trusted advisor to elected officials, corporate and non-profit executives.

John served as director of corporate communications for Rolls-Royce Corporation. At Rolls-Royce, John was responsible for integrated marketing communications, including internal and external communications, media relations, trade shows and exhibits, state and local government relations, community relations, branding, visual communications and corporate social responsibility. He was the lead communications executive on the crisis communications planning and implementation committee, as well as, the primary spokesperson for Rolls-Royce. John served on the board of the political action committee (PAC) and was responsible for corporate social responsibility (CSR) planning and contributions.

Earlier, John served as a corporate officer and vice president for Arvin Inc. (ArvinMeritor), one of the largest global automotive parts manufacturers with more than half of its revenues and profits derived from outside of the United States. At Arvin, John was responsible for integrating investor relations, marketing, corporate communications, public relations, community relations, government relations, graphics and public affairs on a global basis. As the top Investor Relations executive for the Company, John was instrumental in helping grow the Company from $350 million to over $7.5 billion. John also served as the President of the Arvin Foundation.

Active in the community, John was elected to four terms on the city council and served as president of the City Council. In addition, he sat on the boards of the Columbus Housing Authority, United Way, Boys and Girls Club, Habitat for Humanity and New American Schools.

After graduating from Ball State University, John started his career by serving in the offices of the Indiana Lt. Governor and Governor; and as a staff member to the Vice-President of the United States, The Honorable George H.W. Bush. John also served on the re-election campaign staff for Reagan-Bush in 1984. Following the election of George H.W. Bush as President of the United States, Indiana's Governor, the Honorable Bob Orr, was named Ambassador to Singapore where John continued to serve as a trusted advisor.

John, and his wife, Katherine, have three grown children. William, lives in Washington DC. Martha and Margaret both live and work in Charlotte, NC. He enjoys yard work, growing more than 45 varieties of hostas and researching his family's history. John is a cancer survivor since 2011 and continues to serve others as an outspoken advocate and fundraiser for cancer research.

Contact Information:
John Brown
Carolinas Independent Automobile Dealers Association
P: (800) 432-4232   E: jbrown@theciada.com

CAROLINAS INDEPENDENT
AUTOMOBILE DEALERS ASSOCIATION

"The only non-profit association representing independent automobile dealers in the Carolinas".

Industry Lobbying/Governmental Affairs
Representation with DMV in North and South Carolina
Dealer Education
Garage Liability Insurance
Dealer Bonds
Dealer Forms
Other Related Dealership Services

"We're On Your Team!"

www.TheCIADA.com
(800) 432-4232 Toll Free
(704) 455-2117 Office

[Page Intentionally Left Blank]

Dealership Compliance With Federal Regulations

Dealership Compliance With Federal Regulations

While much is said these days about the requirements on dealers to maintain a high level of compliance with any number of federal government rules and regulations, not all dealers are taking heed. Unfortunately, the outcome and/or consequences for non-compliance can be devastating.

In this section, we seek to expose you to some of the compliance requirements. At a minimum, a new dealer should be prepared to examine his/her dealership model to determine which of these rules and regulations apply. It is important to note that while this information is being provided, the best practice is to consult with an industry professional that specializes in compliance or an attorney who focuses on these kinds of issues.

There does not appear to be a requirement that a dealership maintain a specific compliance program, but depending on the dealership operation, said dealership may be subject to many different pieces of legislation that would result in a compliance program. So as a matter of explanation, imagine the requirement is that you maintain a compliance notebook with all of the records necessary to be compliant. If that were so, what would be included in the notebook? Under many of the federal rules the content would hinge on the complexity of your operation and types of practices in use at the dealership. There is no "boiler plate" example, no "one size fits all" book. However, you may find this template explanation as a good place to start. Here are some recommendations as to how to build that notebook.

You will need a 1-inch, 3-ring binder with eight numbered tabs inside. Behind each tab you will place a plan, a document, or evidence of employee training.

Here is a proposed table of contents:

Tab 1 Consumer Privacy Notice
Tab 2 Safeguard Plan
Tab 3 Training Records for your employees on Safeguard Plan
Tab 4 Red Flag Plan
Tab 5 Training Records for your employees on Red Flag Plan
Tab 6   Risk-based Pricing Notice
Tab 7   FIN-CEN-IRS 8300 Form/Cash Collection Policy
Tab 8 Miscellaneous

For each tab you will need to determine if your dealership is required to be compliant with the related regulation, and if so, prepare the necessary documents.

Tab 1 Consumer Privacy Notice

This is a requirement for dealers who obtain personal non-public information from customers in the normal conduct of a financing transaction. The Fair Credit Reporting Act maintains that disclosure to the customer must be given under some instances, especially relating to the release of information to non-affiliated entities. At a minimum, the dealer must prepare and give certain customers a consumer privacy notice, which indicates to the customer the ways in which the dealers may share the personal information supplied by the customer. Furthermore, if the dealership is supplying the financing and it actually finances a deal for a term of at least 12 months, a renewal copy of this notice must be sent to the customer. The customers must be given an "Opt Out" provision with these notices. The Consumer Privacy Notice

Form should reflect the FTC designed form. You may access this form by logging onto the FTC website at www.ftc.gov and look for instructions for using the Privacy Notice Online Form Builder to create a form for your dealership.

Tab 2 Safeguard Plan

The Graham-Leach-Bliley Act, along with its Safeguard Rule, requires that a dealership maintain a plan/procedure/process for protecting personal, non-public information obtained from customers. The program should reflect reasonable practices that make it difficult or impossible for someone to obtain information about a customer if they are not supposed to have access to that information. The rule further mandates that each dealership will appoint a Safeguard Coordinator to oversee and/or supervise the Safeguard Plan. The rule requires a written plan outlining the procedures in place at the dealership that protects customer information. Think simple and plan effective steps. For example, shred documents when you no longer need them (in accordance with state and federal laws), lock files and other documents with customer information on them in file cabinets and limit access to computers that contain customer information. Check references on employees, back up your files in safe locations and insure your plan identifies what steps will be taken if and when your Safeguard Plan is breached.

Tab 3 Training Records for Employees on Safeguard Plan

Providing evidence that your Safeguard Plan has been trained upon is important. You should conduct training with all your employees and have them sign a statement indicating they will comply with the Safeguard Plan.

Tab 4 Red Flag Plan

The Fair and Accurate Credit Transactions Act of 2003 maintains that certain businesses including independent automobile dealers must develop, implement and administer an Identity Theft Prevention Program. The program must include four basic elements- to identify, detect, prevent and mitigate against identity theft. The plan should consist of reasonable policies and procedures to identify "red flags" you might run across in the day-to-day operation of your dealership. These reasonable procedures must be compiled in a written plan.

Furthermore, a dealership must train all employees and keep current training records. The plan must be evaluated on some periodic basis. This scheduled review should be identified in the plan. The supervision of the Red Flag Plan is required to be at the Board of Directors or Senior Management Level. You will not be able to "pass the buck" on this one. You, the dealer, are ultimately in charge and responsible for implementation of this plan. To learn more about your requirements under the Red Flag Rule, go to www.ftc.gov/idtheft.

Tab 5 Training Records for Employees on Red Flag Plan
This tab is where you must maintain your training records for the Red Flag Plan. You should maintain accurate records for each employee that include a written/dated statement by each indicating he/she has read the plan and agrees to comply.

Tab 6 Risk-Based Pricing Notice
The Risk-Based Pricing Notice is a disclosure requirement regarding the practice of risk-based pricing in your dealership. The Federal Reserve Board (FRB) and Federal Trade Commission (FTC) govern compliance for notification. Risk-based pricing is the practice of pricing loans and products based on a customer's credit score. The model works like this- the higher the credit score, the more favorable the rates and terms. A low credit score would receive less favorable rates and terms. A minimum requirement for disclosure under this rule is if you pull a credit score on a customer, you must give them a risk-based pricing notice. Consult your credit bureau for instructions on how to get needed data to

include on a notice for each score you pull. Or if you use dealer management software, the system can be configured to provide you a notice when a score is requested from a credit reporting bureau. Also, you should consult the FTC website at www.ftc.gov for specific requirements. Not all dealership are required to give risk-based pricing notices, but failure to comply if you are required can be expensive.

Tab 7 Fin-Cen-IRS 8300 Rule/Cash Collection Policy

The USA Patriot Act, passed following the horrific events surrounding 9-11-2001, now requires that dealerships and others must report all cash transactions in excess of $10,000.00. Each dealership must have a stated cash collection policy reflecting the process in use at the dealership.

This rule pertains to any single cash transaction of more than $10,000.00 or any two or more related transactions that total more than $10,000.00. The particulars with the rule can be tricky, so a dealership should not take risks in complying. A qualifying transaction must be reported within 15 days of the transaction. By January 31st of the following year, you must also notify the affected person that the form was filed. The rule is very clear as to what is considered cash, as well as, other monetary instruments that are not covered under the rule. Suspicious transactions must be reported using the Form 8300. Customer notification is not required for suspicious transactions. Make sure when reporting under this rule that you use the current version of the Form 8300. The form is dated in the upper left hand corner. At the time of this printing, the current form is dated July 2012. This form may also be reported electronically by going to the IRS website. All Form 8300s, which are reported to the IRS, must be maintained in your dealership files for a period of 5 years. Prior to collecting cash at your dealership, consult www.irs.gov for more details on the Fin-Cen-IRS 8300 Form reporting requirements.

Tab 8 Miscellaneous

Behind Tab 8 you may keep support material for all of the above referenced plans and rules. Additionally, the regulatory environment is dynamic. Therefore, as new rules and regulations are passed down, you will find this tab as an area in your compliance notebook to store information about new and additional regulations.

This section does not address all of the federal rules under which a dealership may be required to comply, but it is a start. Dealerships should also be aware of the requirements under the Equal Credit Opportunity Act, USA Patriot Act, Used Car Rule, Regulation Z-The Truth in Lending Act and Regulation M-The Consumer Leasing Act.

Of particular concern is the prohibition of entering into transactions with a person whose name is on the blocked persons list or the SDN list. The Office of Foreign Assets Control (OFAC), a division of the United States Department of Treasury, maintains the SDN list. People from all over the world can be on this list for a variety of reasons, to include tax evasion, drug cartel activity, and of course, terrorist activity. Business entities are also on this list. At your dealership, you must maintain evidence that you are regularly checking your potential customers against this list. It is virtually impossible to check this list in printed form as it is over 900 pages in length and is regularly updated. The online searches are the most effective means for maintaining compliance in this area. You may go to www.ustreas.gov or www.instantofac.com, to obtain a report on a potential customer.

Now that this exercise is complete, you have a compliance notebook. What's next? Keep the notebook close by. Consult it frequently to make sure it is current with your dealership operations. Penalties under many of the above reference regulations can be as high as $16,000.00 per violation. Regulators are increasing efforts to insure that independent dealerships are compliant.

SPARE PARTS...NOTES

APPENDIX A:

Abbreviations, Aycronyms, and Annectotes

ACV-Actual Cash Value

BHPH- Buy Here Pay Here

LHPH- Lease Here Pay Here

NIADA- National Independent Automobile Dealers Association

NADA- National Automobile Dealers Association (Franchise)

CIADA-Carolina Independent Automobile Dealers Association

DMS- Dealer Management Software

GPS- Global Positioning System

IRS- Internal Revenue Service

DOR- Department of Revenue

DOT- Department of Transportation

DMV- Department of Motor Vehicles

OFAC- Office of Foreign Assets Control

VIN-Vehicle Identification Number

ELT- Electronic Lien and Title System

SUV- Sports Utility Vehicle

CFPB- Consumer Financial Protection Bureau

FTC- Federal Trade Commission

UCC- Uniform Commerical Code

VSC- Vehicle Service Contracts

CPO- Certified Pre-owned

OEM- Original Equipment Manufacturer

DCC- Debt Cancellation Coverage

NICB- National Insurance Crime Bureau

CRM- Customer Relationship Management

ROI- Return on Investment

Reg Z- Truth In Lending Act

Reg M- Consumer Leasing Act

MVR- 608- Gross Vehicle Declaration (North Carolina DMV Form)

MVR-330- Application for a Registration Plate or Transfer of a Registered Plate for a Non-owner/lessee (North Carolina DMV)

PAS- Payment Assurance System

DPPA- Drivers Privacy Protection Act

NMVTIS- National Motor Vehicle Title Information Service

DOJ- Department of Justice

AAMVA- American Association of Motor Vehicle Administrators

Recommended Documents to Retain in a Vehicle Deal File/Jacket

Photo of Vehicle Title (Front and Back)

Photocopy of Dealer Reassignment (if applicable)

Photocopy of Odometer Mileage Disclosure

Photocopy of Damage Disclosure

Photocopy of Vehicle Inspection Receipt (if applicable)

Buyers Order or Bill of Sale

Photocopy of the Buyers Drivers License or I D Card (depends on the state you operate in)

Photocopy of the temporary tag receipt

Repair and/or parts receipts

Financing agreement (if applicable)

Warranty agreement (if applicable)

Floor plan agreement (if applicable)

Consignment agreement (if applicable)

APPENDIX C
New Dealer Checklist

❏ Identify potential dealership location

❏ Contact your state DMV and get the name and phone number of your local inspector... call the inspector early in your process

❏ Check with local (city or county) zoning/planning office to verify that your desired location is zoned appropriately. Find out if there are regulations regarding size/number of signs, landscaping, handicapped access (Americans With Disabilities Act), bathrooms, etc.

❏ Get a copy of your credit report and clean up any items or errors timely

❏ If you plan to incorporate, file articles of incorporation with the appropriate state agency, usually the Secretary of State 's office

❏ If you are confident you will qualify for a bond based on your credit report, lease or purchase property before applying for business license, bond insurance, etc. If you are unsure if you qualify for a bond, contact a qualified insurance agent for assistance

❏ Apply for a surety bond and garage liability insurance (as required in your state)

❏ Apply for all required business/privilege licenses for the municipalities in which you dealership will be located

❏ If required in your state, complete a background check on the principle owners of the dealership or for the person in whose name the dealership license will be issued

❏ File for a Certificate of Occupancy, if required by your city or county

❏ Contact the Department of Labor in your state and procure the necessary state and federal labor law posters

❏ Consult with an accountant to determine what federal, state, and local taxes you will be required to pay or report

❏ Design and post a sign bearing the name of your dealership in compliance with your state rules

❏ Some states require state sales tax licenses. Check with your Department of Revenue to make sure you have all the necessary filings

❏ Obtain a dealers license application from your DMV and complete the form, attached all required documents, have your inspector review and if required sign off on your application prior to sending the application to your DMV

This is a list of recommended actions. There may be additional requirements for new dealers in your state. Always confirm with your state DMV office or consult your independent automobile dealers association

CONTRIBUTING AUTHORS:

MARTY COATES Co-founder and President, Waymaker Learning Corporation

CHRIS MARTIN President/Owner, Team E-Z Auto

BARRY "CHIP" COOPER, JR. President, Commercial Software, Inc. (ComSoft)

MICHAEL SAMAAN Dealer Services Manager, Auto Data Direct, Inc.

ROD HEASLEY President and CRO (Chief Relationships Officer), KISS Concepts Group LLC

TIM BYRD Founder/President, DealerRE, a Tim Byrd & Associates Company

BILLY THREADGILL Co-Owner, Van's Auto Sales, Senior Vice President, NIADA

RUSS ALGOOD CEO, Ace Motor Acceptance Corporation (AMAC)

BOB EARLE South Atlantic Regional Director , NextGear Capital

R. ALLEN DOUGLAS Founder/President , STARS GPS

JOHN BROWN Executive Director, CIADA

This book is published as a joint project between

To learn more or to order additional copies of the book, you may contact any of the contributing authors, CIADA or Waymaker Learning Corporation.

[Page Intentionally Left Blank]